Professor Jennie Batchelor

Jennie is Head and Professor of English at the University of York. She previously worked at the University of Kent for nearly twenty years where she co-directed the Centre for Studies in the Long Eighteenth Century. Prior to that, she was the inaugural Postdoctoral Fellow in Women's Writing (1660-1830) at Chawton House Library and the University of Southampton.

Jennie has a career-long commitment to public engagement in research, and in addition to giving numerous keynote lectures internationally, is regularly interviewed about her research on numerous podcasts, BBC radio and television and has written for various magazines from *The Quilter* to *Who Do You Think You Are* Magazine. In the last five years, Jennie has also become involved in practice-based research on craft reconstruction and craft and mental health which led to her co-creation, with Alison Larkin, of the popular history-craft book, *Jane Austen Embroidery* (Pavilion and Dover, 2020).

First published in the UK in 2025 by Supernova Books, an imprint of Aurora Metro Publications Ltd. 80 Hill Rise, Richmond, TW10 6UB www.aurorametro.com info@aurorametro.com

X: @aurorametro F: facebook.com/AuroraMetroBooks

Encounters with Jane Austen: celebrating 250 years copyright © 2025 Aurora Metro Publications Ltd.

Introduction copyright © 2025 Jennie Batchelor

Editing and compilation copyright © 2025 Cheryl Robson. Assisted by Emma Hawes and Caitlin Grills.

Cover design: copyright © 2025 Aurora Metro Publications Ltd.

Individual contributors retain the copyright in their own works.

Afterword by Julia Quinn, copyright © 2008 Julia Quinn; from *Mansfield Park* by Jane Austen, with introduction by Margaret Drabble and an afterword by Julia Quinn. Used by permission of Signet, an imprint of Penguin Publishing Group, a division of PRH LLC. All rights reserved.

Photographs and illustrations are included with permission, under creative commons licence or are in the public domain. [Line-drawings by Hugh Thomson from the 1894 edition of *Pride & Prejudice*.]

All rights are strictly reserved. For rights enquiries please contact the publisher: info@aurorametro.com

No part of this publication may be reproduced, stored in or introduced into a retrieval system, or transmitted in any form, or by any means (electronic, mechanical, photocopying, recording or otherwise) without the prior permission of the publisher. Any person who does any unauthorised act in relation to this publication may be liable to criminal prosecution and civil claims for damages. The publisher prohibits use of the work for purposes of training artificial intelligence technologies to generate text, including without limitation, technologies that are capable of generating works in the same style or genre as the work.

This paperback is sold subject to the condition that it shall not, by way of trade or otherwise, be lent, resold, hired out, or otherwise circulated without the publisher's prior consent in any form of binding or cover other than that in which it is published and without a similar condition being imposed on the subsequent purchaser.

Printed by Short Run Press, UK, on sustainably resourced paper.
ISBNs: 978-1-913641-51-1 (print)
978-1-913641-52-8 (ebook)

Encounters with Jane Austen

celebrating 250 years

introduced by
Jennie Batchelor

compiled and edited by
Cheryl Robson

SUPERNOVA BOOKS

About the editor:

Cheryl Robson is the founder of award-winning independent publisher Aurora Metro, a finalist for Small Press of the Year 2025 in the British Book Awards. Aurora Metro is home to the popular culture imprint Supernova Books and the drama imprint Amber Lane Press. 2025 also sees the launch of new non-fiction humanities imprint River Light Press with co-publisher Lucy Melville.

Cheryl has been shortlisted for the ITV National Diversity Awards for both Lifetime Achievement and as an Entrepreneur. Aurora Metro has been shortlisted twice for the Independent Publisher Guild's national awards for diversity in publishing.

Cheryl is also an award-winning playwright, editor and filmmaker but is perhaps best-known for her successful campaign to commission and erect a bronze statue in honour of Virginia Woolf which was unveiled in Richmond, Surrey, in 2022 and has become a favoured tourist attraction close to the publishers' offices and bookshop, Books on the Rise.

Other books in this series:

Encounters with James Baldwin; celebrating 100 years
ISBN 9781913641412 £15.99

Encounters with Marilyn Monroe: celebrating 100 years
ISBN 978-1-913641-55-9 £15.99

Contents

Timeline	7
Introduction by Jennie Batchelor	10
My Good Friend Jane by Katherine Reay	30
Charlotte by Talulah Riley	38
How to find a Partner in Oxford by Kimberley Bailey	49
A Role Model for Women's Solidarity by Emily Midorikawa and Emma Claire Sweeney	53
She by Zita Holbourne	57
Georgiana Darcy – Pistols at Dawn by Julia Miller	62
Discovering Pride in Austen's Time by Caitlin Grills	78
Three of Diamonds by Stephanie Lyttle	86
Mansfield Park essay by Julia Quinn	88
A Zuihitsu on Various Walks by Ellora Sutton	97
First Impressions [extract] by Charlie Lovett	108
Tom Lefroy devours a Cotillion by Marcelle Newbold	114
Kipling's Tribute to Austen by Mary Hamer	118
Buried Love by Sara Teasdale	126
Staging Persuasion Interview with director Jeff James	130
Meeting with Jane by April de Angelis	143
She played and sang: Jane Austen and Music Interview with Gillian Dooley and Jennie Batchelor	152
A Slow-burn Love Story by Katie Lumsden	166
Words that blink by Esme Gutch	173
Jane Austen and Shelley in the Garden [extracts] by Janet Todd	174

Untitled by Karenjit Sandhu	184
Sculpting Jane Interview with Martin Jennings	189
Witch-Wife by Edna St. Vincent Millay	198
Jane Austen and the Gothic Novel by Ellen Cheshire	200
Love's Armour by Allyson Joule	213
The Completion Competition by Natalie Jenner	214
Austen's Onscreen Evolution by Jen Francis	226
Shedding Skin by Jurie Jean van de Vyver	237
The Jane Austen Festival by Rachel Beswick	242
Austen's World Photographs	244

"There are as many forms of love as there are moments in time."

– Jane Austen

Timeline

16 December 1775

Jane Austen is born in Hampshire.

1787 – 1794

Jane writes *Love and Friendship* (1790), *Lesley Castle* (1792) and *Lady Susan* (1794).

1795

Jane writes *Elinor and Marianne,* later to become *Sense and Sensibility.*

1796 – 1797

Jane writes *First Impressions*, which is later published as *Pride and Prejudice.* Her father offers it to a publisher, but it is rejected.

1798 – 1799

Jane writes *Susan* (later published as *Northanger Abbey*).

1801

Jane, her father, her mother, and Cassandra leave Steventon and move to Bath.

December 1802

Jane accepts an offer of marriage from Harris Bigg-Wither, the rich brother of her friends, but declines the next day.

1803

Susan is sold by brother Henry's lawyer to a publisher for £10, but not published.

January 1805

Jane's father dies suddenly, leaving Jane, Cassandra, and their mother poor and dependent on their brothers.

1806

Jane, Cassandra, and their mother move to Southampton to live with Jane's brother Frank and his wife.

July 1809

Jane and Cassandra move to Chawton Cottage with their mother.

Encounters with Jane Austen

1811

Sense and Sensibility is published anonymously 'By A Lady'.

1813

Pride and Prejudice is published 'by the author of *Sense and Sensibility*'.

1814

Mansfield Park is published.

December 1815

Emma is published.

1816

Jane's brother, Henry, buys back the manuscript of *Susan* for £10.

1815 – 1816

Jane writes *The Elliots* (later published as *Persuasion*). She becomes ill but continues to write.

January 1817

Jane begins *The Brothers* (later published as *Sanditon*) but does not complete it.

April 1817

Jane's illness confines her to bed. In her will, she leaves nearly everything to her 'dearest Sister Cassandra'.

May 1817

Jane moves with Cassandra to Winchester for medical treatment.

18 July 1817

Jane dies in Winchester, age 41. She is buried in Winchester Cathedral.

December 1817

Northanger Abbey and *Persuasion* are published. Jane Austen is identified as the author for the first time.

1869

The first biography of Jane, *A Memoir of Jane Austen*, written by her nephew James Edward Austen-Leigh, is published.

1825

Sanditon is published under the title *Fragment of a Novel*.

Jane Austen (1775-1817) engraving from 1873 by unknown artist. Published in *Portrait Gallery of Eminent Men and Women with Biographies,* USA, 1873.

Introduction

Jennie Batchelor

> Oh! it is only a novel ... or, in short, only some work in which the greatest powers of the mind are displayed, in which the most thorough knowledge of human nature, the happiest delineation of its varieties, the liveliest effusions of wit and humour are conveyed to the world in the best chosen language.
>
> – Jane Austen, *Northanger Abbey* (1818)

A few months after her death in July 1817, Jane Austen finally received public acknowledgement as a novelist. The edition of *Northanger Abbey* and *Persuasion* that appeared posthumously at the end of that year opened with a brief 'Biographical Notice' by her brother Henry, which for the first time named his sister as the author of *Sense and Sensibility* (1811), *Pride and Prejudice* (1813), *Mansfield Park* (1814) and *Emma* (1816). 'Short and easy', he wrote, was his task as biographer. 'A life of usefulness, literature, and religion, was not by any means a life of event.'[1]

A life of no event. The irony of Henry's words is truly Austenian. How could he characterise the life and career of one of the most famous writers of all time as non-events? Today, Jane Austen is one of the most translated, adapted and written about authors. Her stories and characters have been retold with the insertion of zombies and sea monsters and transplanted to India, Beverley Hills high schools and Fire

---

[1] Henry Austen, 'Biographical Notice of the Author', in *Northanger Abbey and Persuasion*, London: John Murray, 1818, p. 3.

Introduction

Island. They have reappeared as dating guides, self-help books and soft porn, while her words have been immortalised on fridge magnets, mugs, t-shirts, stationery and tote bags. Jane Austen is a global brand. Her work has twice inspired sets of British postage stamps (in 1975 and 2013), and since 2017 she has been the face of the British £10 note, becoming only the third writer (after Shakespeare and Dickens) to appear on a UK banknote. Even Henry would have acknowledged that his sister's afterlives have been eventful. Jane Austen, we assume, would have been baffled, if amused.

The majority of the Austen siblings – Jane was one of eight – lived into their seventies and beyond. Her life was cut short, however. Who knows what direction her career would have taken had she not died, aged forty-one, of a painful illness that was possibly Addison's disease or Hodgkins Lymphoma? But was her relatively short life a quiet and uneventful one? Austen never married and turned down what seems to have been the only marriage proposal she received from the wealthy, dull Harris Bigg-Wither. She had some independent income from publishing the four novels that appeared before her death. Yet, like her sister and mother, she was largely financially dependent on male relatives. Although she regularly visited her wealthy sibling, Edward Austen Knight, at his impressive, Pemberley-like estate of Godmersham, Kent, she was only a visitor to the big houses of her relatives and observed them with an insight only outsiders possess. Her happiest years were spent in the sociable yet small village of Chawton in Hampshire. She never reconciled herself fully to the bustle of cities such as Bath, Southampton and Winchester to which she was driven for short spells by financial necessity or ill health. She made good use of these experiences in her fiction, however.

Yet uneventful is the last word that comes to mind when thinking about Austen's spirited and productive life, a life lived against the backdrop of revolutions, military conflicts, economic crises, political scandals and debates on humanitarian issues including the rights of men and women and the abolition of the transatlantic slave trade. For years after her death, Austen readers and scholars thought she lived oblivious to such events and distanced her fiction from them to focus on the social dynamics that underpinned or threatened friendships, families and communities. Winston Churchill famously re-read her novels during World War Two to remind himself of an England unmarked by the devastation through which his generation was living. A similar impulse plays out in Rudyard Kipling's short story, 'The Janeites' (1924), which follows a group of soldiers who form a secret Jane Austen society – two decades before the now international Jane Austen Society was founded in 1940 – as they navigate the horrors and aftermath of World War One.

Many of Austen's readers have found comfort in her novels in difficult times. I have been reading her since I was ten. Overwhelming worry and exhaustion meant I could barely read the ingredients list on a tin of tomatoes when my son was born prematurely. But I did find consolation in re-reading *Persuasion*, which saw me through six weeks of neonatal care – my slowest Austen read. Then in March 2020, when forced to leave my office before the Covid-19 pandemic and wondering which of my books, papers and student-purchased gifts I should take home, I simply scooped up the seven volumes of the complete Austen. Like Churchill and Kipling, I suppose, I knew I would find solace in her brilliantly crafted and witty fiction. Yet I found (and still find) this escapism powerful because it seems to me to come from a place of wisdom, not denial, about how the turbulence of the world ripples through our lives.

The busyness of Jane Austen's own life was evident from the start. She was born on 16 December 1775 in Steventon, Hampshire, where her father was rector. Jane was the seventh child born to Reverend George and Cassandra Austen (née

Introduction

Leigh) and the couple's second daughter. Aside from the Austen siblings, the rectory was populated by male boarders whom George educated to supplement his clerical income. Many of these pupils were destined for university, like Jane's brothers, James and Henry, who followed their father to St John's College, Oxford. The majority, her brothers included, were educated for the professions. Francis and Charles went on to have distinguished naval careers, while Henry served in the militia, tried his hand (unsuccessfully) at banking, and later became a clergyman like their brother, James. Edward, meanwhile, was taken under the wing of the family's wealthy cousins, the Knights. After being made their heir, he took on the Knight name and inherited three large estates in Kent and Hampshire. Only her brother George, who seems to have experienced seizures and suffered from cognitive and possibly physical disabilities, did not secure an independent living. He lived outside the family home in a neighbouring village and died in 1838 in his early seventies.

Although they were close to their brothers, early life for Jane and her sister Cassandra was different. Both girls had little formal education. A short spell at Mrs Cawley's school in Southampton in 1783 was cut short when Jane contracted typhus. Two years later, they spent eighteen months in Reading at the boarding school of Madame LaTournelle, whose legal name was the prosaic-sounding Sarah Hackitt. The Abbey School curriculum prioritised skills for acquiring a husband or running a household, including reading, writing, arithmetic, needlework, drawing and dancing. It was not one the girls followed for long before they returned home. Their parents could no longer afford the school fees.

Beyond these sporadic periods of formal education, Austen acquired her knowledge of the world within the comfort of Steventon Rectory and through visits from her many friends and large extended family. It was a home filled with people, books, readings and performances, or 'private theatricals', in which plays were acted out by the Austens in the barn in the summer or dining room in the winter.

Throughout her life, Austen was a voracious reader of novels, poetry, plays and periodicals. She started writing herself at the age of eleven, turning her hand to poetry, short fiction and a witty, concise 'History of England', complete with watercolour portraits by Cassandra, a talented amateur artist. Nearly thirty pieces of Austen's youthful works are preserved in three notebooks, in which she transcribed about 90,000 words of material between 1787 and 1793. These teenage writings are still not as widely read as her later novels. Anyone picking any of them up for the first time is likely to be as shocked as delighted by their rambunctious style. Drunkenness, suicide, theft, murder, flirtation, over-consumption of ice cream, seduction and even cannibalism feature in these riotous fictions, which were written for her family's entertainment and contained a cast of characters loosely inspired by them.

Superficially, novellas like 'Jack and Alice', 'Frederic and Elfrida' and 'The Beautifull Cassandra' – misspellings litter the manuscripts – seem worlds away from Austen's later novels. But the connections are there. We find in them the origins of her more spirited heroines, like Marianne Dashwood, Lydia Bennet and Mary Crawford, as well as the foundations for the more scandalous seduction plotlines that orbit around her central courtship plots. We also see Austen experimenting – sometimes to extremes – with a verbal economy she later turned into an art form. In *Persuasion*, it is hard to think of a word you can cut without losing something important. In 'The Beautifull Cassandra', each chapter is just a couple of sentences long.

We can also see in the teenage writings how much Austen understood the literary tastes of the day and how much fun she had in both revelling in and sending up the conventions of the sentimental novel, especially its effusions of feeling

Introduction

and overblown language. This is especially evident in the two epistolary fictions she wrote. 'Love and Freindship' (sic) was written in 1790, months after the storming of the Bastille. A wildly improbable tale, narrated via a series of letters, it was dedicated to Jane's glamorous cousin, Eliza de Feuillide (née Hancock). Eliza, who had been born in India in 1761, was married to the wealthy Jean-François Capot de Feuillide, who claimed to be a Count and was guillotined in 1794. Eliza, with whom Jane was fascinated, later became Henry's wife. Eliza may also have provided inspiration for the title character of Austen's most technically accomplished early work, *Lady Susan*. Probably written in 1794, *Lady Susan* is an extraordinary novel, not least because of the vivid, intelligent, widowed Lady Susan herself who flirts outrageously and toys mercilessly with the feelings of her daughter as she schemes for personal advantage. For a writer whose novels often feature dead or otherwise lacking maternal figures, Lady Susan wins the prize for Austen's worst mother.

Her family life was much happier, not least because her writing ambitions were encouraged. But it would be wrong to present life at Steventon as an uncomplicated idyll. Death was part of life's fabric, and in 1795, Jane's sister-in-law, Anne (James's wife) died, leaving Jane's niece, Anna, without a mother. Events on the world stage, particularly war with the newly republican France, were also felt keenly by English families, especially those with loved ones in the military. In 1793, the Austens were relieved that Francis safely returned five years after setting sail for the East Indies. The following year, Charles left to go to sea, only to be followed the next year by Tom Fowle, Cassandra's fiancée, who was chaplain on a West Indian campaign. In 1797, Tom died of a fever and was buried at sea. Cassandra never married.

Life took another turn in 1801 when George Austen retired from the clergy. Since the family home at Steventon was tied to his living, George, his wife and daughters had to relocate. They went to Bath where Austen's parents had married in 1764 and her maternal uncle and aunt, the wealthy Leigh Perrots, had a residence in addition to a country estate in Berkshire. Tradition has it that news of having to move to Bath caused Jane Austen to faint, though the story might be apocryphal. The few surviving letters she wrote from Bath at this time suggest she was interested in the comings and goings and trappings of this most fashionable of cities, but this was a lean period of new writing in Austen's life.

In the five years before leaving Steventon, Austen completed drafts of three novels: 'First Impressions' (later published as *Pride and Prejudice*), 'Elinor and Marianne' (later *Sense and Sensibility*) and 'Susan' (later *Northanger Abbey*). Early drafts of these novels have not survived and details of their composition history are murky. It seems likely, though, that 'Elinor and Marianne' and possibly 'First Impressions' were originally written in the epistolary style, as a series of letters. Whatever their form, early versions of both were circulated among and enjoyed by Jane's family members and close friends. But Austen had her sights set on broader circulation. In 1797, her father tried to secure the interest of publisher Thomas Cadell in 'First Impressions', though he did not disclose its author's identity. Cadell declined the novel we know as *Pride and Prejudice* by return of post without looking at it.

We don't know how Austen felt about this setback, but she remained undaunted and revised 'Susan' in 1802 while in Bath, the city in which much of *Northanger Abbey* is set. A year later, she sold the copyright for the novel to publisher Benjamin Crosby in a deal negotiated anonymously via Henry. Unfortunately, Crosby sat on the manuscript and never published it. An irate Austen later tried to retrieve her novel, but it took her until 1816 to muster the spare £10 needed to buy it back, and even then she borrowed the money from Henry.

Introduction

It was not until 1803 or 1804 that Austen began a new novel entitled 'The Watsons', about 7,500 words of which exist in draft. Certain of the novel's characters and plots will be familiar to Austen fans. The Watsons are a large family, headed by their widowed and ailing clergyman father. The heroine, Emma, has been raised and educated by a wealthy relative, but returns to live with her family following her aunt's marriage, whereupon a ball introduces her to an aristocratic family and various courtship possibilities. More than any of Austen's other novels, the spectre of financial precarity weighs heavily in 'The Watsons', forcing Emma to contemplate paid work as a teacher in a way that only *Emma*'s Jane Fairfax does before being spared by marriage to the capricious Frank Churchill. We will never know if Emma Watson was to share a similar fate. Various reasons have been suggested for why Austen never completed the novel. James Edward Austen-Leigh speculated that his aunt might have felt she had placed her heroine 'too low'.[2] It's more likely that the sudden death of her father in January 1805 left Jane unable to complete her new work.

For the next four years, Austen, her mother and sister led a peripatetic life. They stayed in Bath for a few months, before moving between Hampshire and Kent, a few months in Worthing, Sussex, and then a longer stay with Francis Austen in Southampton. It wasn't until 1809 that the Austen women were finally settled and only then because of the intervention of another of her brothers. This time Edward provided assistance by offering a cottage in the grounds of one of his Hampshire estates in Chawton, near Alton. The residence – now Jane Austen's House – was Austen's much-loved home until shortly before her death, and lived in by Cassandra until she died in 1845.

It was at Chawton that Austen revised or wrote from scratch all of her six completed novels. Her first, *Sense and*

---

2 J. E. Austen–Leigh, *A Memoir of Jane Austen*, London: Richard Bentley and Son, 1871, p. 364.

Encounters with Jane Austen

Sensibility, appeared just two years after settling there, in an anonymous publishing deal again brokered by Henry. *Sense and Sensibility* is a novel about the displacement and financial insecurity of the Dashwood sisters and their mother after their father's death and their step-brother's refusal to provide for them. Gone was the epistolary structure of the original 'Elinor and Marianne', but, as in many of her novels where they are often used to reveal the true feelings and characters of men, letters remain an important plot driver. Quite how much of the 1790s draft remains in the finished novel is unclear, but it is possible that the subplot of Colonel Brandon's deceased first love, Eliza, abandoned to poverty by his brother and left to raise an illegitimate daughter later seduced by the charismatic Willoughby, is a remnant from this time. Many novels from the 1790s contained similar seduction plots. *Sense and Sensibility* was a success. It earned Austen around £140 and the original print run sold out by 1813, the year in which *Pride and Prejudice* appeared.

Pride and Prejudice remains Austen's best known and most adapted work. In a novel that fizzes with brilliantly drawn characters, from tedious Mary and ridiculous Mrs Bennet to self-important Lady Catherine, obsequious Mr Collins and rakish Wickham, Elizabeth Bennet and Mr Darcy have always seemed to have a life of their own. When visiting a Royal Academy exhibition in London in 1813, Austen joked that she regretted not seeing a portrait that looked like her much-loved heroine. The story of Lizzy Bennet's rise from prospective financial precarity to marriage to the wealthy Darcy seems like the stuff of fairy tales and has inspired hundreds of enemies-to-lovers romances since. Quite whether the novel is as fairy-tale like or romantic as Colin Firth (whether as wet-shirt clad Mr Darcy or as Bridget Jones's Mark Darcy) implies is a moot point. When Lizzy visits Darcy's estate, after having turned down his marriage proposal, she falls in love. But it's not clear whether her head and heart are turned by the man or the mansion. Lizzy Bennet is not the only one of Austen's heroines

Introduction

to fall in love with a man's house around the same time that she seems to fall in love with its owner. To be 'mistress of Pemberley' (not Darcy, note) really would 'be something!'[3]

The country house comes under a different kind of scrutiny in *Mansfield Park*, which follows Fanny Price, the daughter of a financially stretched naval family. At the age of ten, Fanny is taken in by her uncle and aunt, the Bertrams, and raised, if unequally, with her cousins. The novel shares a conventional courtship plot with the heroine eventually marrying one of her cousins after less acceptable matches are (mostly) thwarted. It also has an array of entertaining characters, from sofa-ridden Lady Bertram to caddish Henry Crawford and his bold sister Mary. Yet *Mansfield Park* is an unsettling novel, both in its depiction of the humiliations Fanny suffers and in the novel's revelation of the colonial underpinnings of the Bertrams' wealth in an Antiguan slave plantation. When Fanny asks her uncle about the 'slave trade', she is met with a 'dead silence' that has haunted readers.[4]

The Austens had complex relationships to the transatlantic slave trade, which had been abolished in 1807, though plantation slavery in British colonies persisted into the 1830s. Her favourite writers included prominent abolitionists such as poet, William Cowper, which perhaps suggests her views on the matter, and as a naval officer, her brother Charles intercepted ships involved in the illegal trafficking in enslaved people post 1807. At the same time, their aunt, Jane Leigh Perrot, was heiress to a plantation in Barbados. In raising the spectre of the slave trade only to be silent on the matter, is *Mansfield Park* complicit with its atrocities? Or does Austen stage a silence on one of the most divisive and urgent matters of her day to provoke conversation in her readers' drawing rooms? We may never know, but what is clear, is that Austen's novels are

---
3 Jane Austen, *Pride and Prejudice*, ed. Pat Rogers, Cambridge: Cambridge University Press, 2006, p. 271.
4 Jane Austen, *Mansfield Park*, ed. John Wiltshire, Cambridge: Cambridge University Press, p. 231

in dialogue with the complex and volatile world in which she lived, no matter what some of her readers have thought.

The same cannot be said of the imaginative world inhabited by the 'handsome, clever, and rich' heroine of Austen's fourth novel.[5] While *Emma* has more labouring characters than any Austen work – not only servants, but farmers and the labouring poor – the heroine spends much of her time indulging in romantic possibilities that are divorced from socio-economic realities. A narcissistic interpreter of the fictional village of Highbury in which she lives with her hypochondriac father, Emma is also lonely and bored after her friend and governess marries, and tries to alleviate these feelings by launching matchmaking schemes for the orphaned, low-born Harriet Smith. *Emma* is a novel about game playing – about the word games we play to pass time with company, the metaphorical games required to navigate polite society or, in the hands of Frank Churchill and Emma, the games we play with people to entertain ourselves. It is her most technically brilliant work and the last novel to be published in her lifetime.

Northanger Abbey and *Persuasion*, published together and posthumously, are an unlikely pairing despite their shared Bath setting. *Northanger Abbey*'s Catherine Morland is youthful and credulous. Set in the 1790s when the novel was originally written and preserving some of the bawdiness of her teenage writing, the novel takes satirical aim at the melodrama of gothic novels which lead Catherine to believe that General Tilney, her future father-in-law, killed his wife. The scene in which a disabused Catherine is forced to face up to the consequences of her overactive imagination is excruciatingly drawn. No one writes humiliation better than Jane Austen. The novel ends happily, but like all of Austen's endings, is unnerving. General Tilney is no murderer, but like Sir Thomas Bertram, he is a tyrannical father and an unpleasant man. The question of how

---

5 Jane Austen, *Emma*, ed. Richard Cronin and Dorothy McMillan, Cambridge: Cambridge University Press, p. 3.

Introduction

Catherine's marriage to his son will work out given all that has gone before is left open.

Anne Elliot, of *Persuasion*, is more mature in age and manners than Catherine. At 27 she is considered to be beyond marriageable age. She lives also with the double regret of having been displaced from her family home after the financial mismanagement of her vain father and of having eight years earlier turned down Frederick Wentworth, a naval officer recently risen through the ranks to become Captain with a cache of prize money to boot. *Persuasion* is the most romantic of Austen's novels and, not coincidentally, there is no big house in offing for Anne who loses her beloved Kellynch at the beginning of the novel and never gets it back (despite what the 2007 ITV adaptation suggests). *Persuasion* also has the most precise historical setting of any Austen novels: the brief cessation in the wars with France in 1814 to 1815 before Napoleon escaped from exile and was defeated at Waterloo. Austen's first readers would have known when Anne and Wentworth marry in the novel's conclusion that the war would soon resume and with devastating consequences. We have to hope that Austen's hero, like her naval brothers, survived. The novel seems unsure.

When Austen herself died in the summer of 1817, she left behind nearly twelve chapters of an unfinished novel. *Sanditon* deserves its reputation as an unfinished masterpiece in the making. Centred on the founding of an upcoming, fictional seaside resort town in Sussex, it feels like a departure for a writer who was moving confidently into new territory. Charlotte Heywood, from whose perspective much of the manuscript is told, is a compelling character, but readers have been equally intrigued by Miss Lambe, a wealthy heiress and the only Austen character to be explicitly of African descent. Austen's fiction always follows the money, and the novel hints that Miss Lambe will be targeted by fortune hunters. We assume she would have played a significant role in the novel and that her money, and the men pursuing it, would have complicated or consolidated her friendship with Charlotte. The hugely popular PBS dramatization of *Sanditon* (2019-2023) opted for the latter possibility and is one in a long line of continuations of the novel, including one (also unfinished) by Austen's niece, Anna Austen Lefroy, from the 1850s.

Jane Austen died in July 1817 in Winchester, to which she relocated in a futile attempt to find a surgeon who might cure her mysterious illness. She never left the city and was buried in the nave of Winchester Cathedral. The memorial stone her brothers commissioned is now a site of pilgrimage to which Austenites flock and documents Austen's personal traits: her kindness, piety and how much she was loved by family and friends. The events of her life and the event of her writing go unmentioned on the stone, an omission remedied in the 1870s when an additional plaque was erected to acknowledge the achievements of one of the most important novelists of all time.

What would Austen have made of her extraordinary afterlives? How would she have reacted to the sales, the adaptations, the festivals, the balls, the banknotes, the tea towels and the road signs declaring Hampshire 'Jane Austen's County'? We can only speculate, a tantalising train of thought April De Angelis pursues here in an imagined dialogue between an 'inscrutable' Jane and De Angelis herself. No doubt some of the ways in which Austen's fiction has been read since her death would have solicited surprise or infuriation. Janet Todd plays with these possibilities in 'Jane Austen and Shelley in the Garden'. Here, Austen's ghost haunts the fictional Fran who confronts the deceased author about various misdemeanours including betraying Fanny Price by marrying her off to Edmund Bertram and the 'caution, civility and repression' of her novels' 'romantic endings'. Austen's (pardon the pun) spirited responses to Fran's misinterpretations are so convincing because Todd captures the devastatingly succinct and arch Austen we know from her novels and especially her correspondence.

Introduction

Sadly, only some of the many letters Austen wrote in her lifetime survived the fire into which her devoted sister threw them following her death. A few are regularly quoted in a bid to prove that Austen was a modest and unambitious writer, a view that contributors to this book refute. In one such letter, dated 16-17 December 1816, Austen famously likened her novels to miniature paintings. In another, dated 1 April 1816, she demurred she couldn't only write a 'Historical Romance' and had to 'go on in my own way'.[6] But context is everything and it is important to note that these self-effacing descriptions were written, respectively, to a boy and a man, who were offering commentary and advice to a novelist who did not want either. The recipient of the latter of these two quips was James Stanier Clarke. He was Librarian to the Prince of Wales, the married yet philandering royal whom Austen hated but to whom she reluctantly dedicated *Emma*. The dedication is discussed in this book by Emily Midorikawa and Emma Claire Sweeney. Their essay also illuminates Austen's solidarity with women, like governess Anne Sharp, who were trying to live in a world characterised by gendered and sexual double standards. It is a kind of solidarity that Julia Miller imagines, here, for Georgiana Darcy in the delightfully retributive 'Pistols at Dawn', in which Wickham finally gets his comeuppance when Georgiana (some time after the events of *Pride and Prejudice*) receives help from a surprising quarter.

The light Austen's fiction sheds on such gendered inequalities is undoubtedly part of its enduring appeal and a theme that runs across several of the poems that appear later in this volume. Modern readers debate how much of a feminist Austen was. It was not a word she would have known and her gender politics were not as radical as those of contemporaries such as Mary Wollstonecraft. But injustice, especially when meted out against women, made Austen 'M.A.D.' (the initials she used when masquerading as Mrs Ashton Dennis when

6 Jane Austen, *Jane Austen's Letters*, ed. Deirdre Le Faye, Oxford: Oxford University Press, 2011, p. 326, 337.

trying to get the unpublished *Susan* back from Crosby). Her novels, like her heroines Catherine Morland, Elizabeth Bennet and Marianne Dashwood, anatomises the patriarchy in ways that, as Zita Holbourne shows us in her poem 'She', continue to resonate with and move us today.

Elsewhere in the letters, we see more of this Austen, an Austen who was acerbic, riotously funny and had ambition. Austen could be self-deprecatory, but her modesty is frequently performative and tinged with irony. It is this Austen who takes centre stage in Charlie Lovett's 'First Impressions'. Here a fictionalised Austen's wry parroting of criticisms that novels are 'full of nonsense' becomes the foundation of a friendship with fellow fiction-lover Reverend Mansfield. Austen shows her love of and fascination with fiction in everything she writes. As Ellen Cheshire discusses in her essay on 'Jane Austen and the Gothic Novel', this is true even when the author parodies the most overblown conventions to press them into the service of a less sensational form of novelistic realism. Indeed, Austen is one of the greatest champions the novel has ever had and not just in the brilliant defense of it in *Northanger Abbey* from which the epigraph to my Introduction is taken. She advocated for the novel most eloquently as a practitioner. As Katie Lumsden discusses in her essay for this book, Austen was a tenacious writer who bounced back from every professional setback and rejection she experienced to refine her works until they finally entered the world in all their technical accomplishment. And technically accomplished they most certainly are. In the words of Jeff James, who is interviewed here about his 2017 modern-dress dramatic adaptation of *Persuasion* for the Manchester Royal Exchange, 'what Jane Austen achieved' in her six novels with their 'formidably structured plots' and rich 'architecture' is 'unparalleled'.

That Austen was a craftswoman and took her craft seriously is a thread woven into the fabric of this book and highlighted beautifully by Stephanie Lyttle's poem, 'Three of Diamonds',

Introduction

which takes inspiration from a diamond quilt Jane made with her mother and sister. 'Like / good sentences / stitches, too, have their syntax', Lyttle writes. Austen was an extremely skilled needlewoman as the few surviving examples of the many items she stitched during her life attest. It is tempting to see parallels between her deft needlecraft and her craft as a writer, or, as Gillian Dooley does in her wide-ranging account of Austen's talents as a singer and piano player, to draw links between her musicianship and the creation of her rhythmical prose and careful orchestration of plots and subplots.

Not all domestic accomplishments were accommodated so neatly to the demands of a writing life, though. Several of the contributions to this book reflect on the challenges Austen faced as a woman writer torn between competing personal and professional demands. Austen occasionally reflected on these challenges in her letters when she contemplated women trying to write with children to look after, houses to manage and leaky guttering to get fixed. Similar tensions are captured by Martin Jennings in his discussion of his dynamic sculpture of Jane Austen, rising from her desk in the face of mundane interruptions. But however much she rose, Austen always went back to her desk until, that is, the moment that her health failed her and she could write no longer. It is at this poignant time in 1817 when we meet Austen in Natalie Jenner's 'The Completion Competition', in which the dying writer imagines who she might choose to take up and finish 'Sanditon' for her.

How must Austen have felt knowing she would not be able to complete what might have been her greatest work? This was a writer, after all, who referred to her novels as her children. Generations of Austen's readers have viewed her characters with a similar sense of intimacy, experiencing what Ellora Sutton aptly describes in this book as a 'very real, almost parasocial' relationship with Austen's fiction and its creator. It is to this same comforting companionship that Katherine Reay looked during a long period of rehabilitation after successive surgeries and found in Elinor Dashwood a character who 'taught me how to hold it together when everything felt like it was falling apart'. Even those characters with whom we don't identify so readily make us want to get to know them. Many readers would probably agree with Julia Quinn that they don't want to be Fanny Price, but that doesn't stop us wanting to understand her, just as we want to know whether *Pride and Prejudice's* pragmatic Charlotte Lucas was right when she told Elizabeth Bennet that pursuing love is a fool's game. Talulah Riley's short story 'Charlotte', in true Austenian and Facebook style, shows that it's complicated when it comes to human relationships. Every life choice has unforeseen repercussions, even for those as clear-sighted as Charlotte Lucas.

Of course, not everyone falls in love with Austen on a first or second reading date, or even after the slow-burn multiple re-readings Lumsden describes. Indeed, sometimes the romance plots of Austen's fiction are precisely what puts readers off. But as we have seen, Jane Austen's novels are not romantic in an uncomplicated way. As Caitlin Grills observes in 'Discovering Pride in Austen's Time', Austen's fiction is more deeply concerned with the consequences people 'face if deemed to be loving inappropriately'. It is this fascination with 'inappropriate' love that has inspired so many queer reworkings of Austen on the page, stage and screen. Such reimaginings are part of a long and varied history of Austen reimaginings that began in the Victorian period and have proliferated ever since. It is an adaptation history that speaks, as Jen Francis discusses, to the distinctive 'adaptability' of a body of work that 'continues to offer a mirror to society' and to ourselves. The very best of these adaptations can change our relationship to Austen's fiction. It is precisely this process that Mary Hamer describes in her account of seeing Austen anew through the lens of Rudyard Kipling's 'The Janeites', a short story that documents the consolation following profound loss experienced by Kipling and his hero Humberstall after reading

Introduction

Austen. Humberstall, Hamer writes, reveals even to those, like herself, who don't consider themselves Austen fans, the 'wonder' of her fiction's 'truthful representation of human behaviour'.

Hamer's, Kipling's and Humberstall's Austens are all different. Perhaps all our Austens are different. As Rachel Beswick writes of the fabulous and popular Jane Austen Festival, held annually in Bath in September, there 'is no one typical Jane Austen Festival-attendee' any more than there is one typical Austen reader. We all encounter Austen differently and from the position of where and when we read her. How we read her changes as the world changes around us. And it is perhaps above all this relentless change that keeps us going back to Jane Austen. She knew that every life was a series of events — some planned, many not. She knew that life was messy and that human relationships bear the weight of the world. Who better, then, to help us navigate that life than Britain's best loved novelist?

"Laugh as much as you choose, but you will not laugh me out of my opinion."

– Pride and Prejudice

"She is tolerable," Darcy said of Elizabeth

My Good Friend Jane

Katherine Reay

After all we've been through, we're on a first name basis – we're friends. Over the years, Jane has given me delightful companionship and a place to rest. She's been an inspiration, a touchpoint, and a mentor. And, over the years – in this seemingly one-sided relationship – I have given her something as well, no matter how small and insignificant it may seem – my thanks, honour, appreciation, and respect.

I first met Jane Austen in 1983 when my mother gave me her masterpiece, *Pride and Prejudice*, for Christmas. I devoured the book and was thrilled to find she'd written five more. Yet, as we all know, after reading those "five more" novels, I felt bereft at the paltry number. We all wish she had lived longer and had been as prolific as Stephen King – but that's a discussion for another day and another essay.

The movie adaptations had to provide that bit "more" for me. Now, remember, this was 1983, so I only had a few available to binge again and again – the 1940 *Pride and Prejudice* with Greer Garson and Laurence Olivier – which despite so many flaws (I'm looking at you, Lady Catherine de Bourgh) – was delightful, as was the 1980 BBC *Pride and Prejudice* miniseries with Elizabeth Garvie. I believe I wore out my VHS tape.

Jane Austen and I went along together like this for almost thirty years. Six novels that I revisited every couple of years, enjoying immensely but thinking about lightly, and a slew of new film adaptations to fulfil that human need for variety. And what a golden age it was for Austen in the movies. I reviewed

My Good Friend Jane

my list of favourites while writing this and counted two adaptations of *Northanger Abbey*, three of *Sense and Sensibility*, four for *Pride and Prejudice*, three for *Mansfield Park*, four for *Emma*, and three for *Persuasion* – and that doesn't include the prodigious number of homages such as *Lost in Austen*, *Bride and Prejudice*, *Clueless*, *Bridget Jones's Diary* and even an episode of *Wishbone* in 1995, *Furst Impressions*. All this bounty before 2009!

My list ends that year because that is when my relationship to Jane Austen changed, and she became simply "Jane." We became close – and she changed my life.

In December 2008, I was severely injured. It took three surgeries during the first months of 2009 to put me back together and several months longer to recover. During much of that time, I could do little more than move from my bed to the sofa at the beginning of the day, and back to my bed at the end. I could not drive my three kids to school nor take them to their after-school activities; I could not stand long enough in the kitchen to make dinner. It was a quiet time, but not necessarily a peaceful one. Those months were filled with physical pain and a lot of anxiety. Would I heal? Would life look the same again? Was this my new "normal"? I incessantly asked all those questions we posit during any crisis or tragedy and, as is the case most of the time, answers did not come.

What I needed was a place in which I could let go of the unanswerable questions and the ever-present anxiety, a place to rest and heal, and I needed friends to sit beside me. Yet real friends were busy – after all, recovery took months – and conversations felt taxing, as all those pesky questions kept coming up. Television felt bland and tedious.

One day I reached for *Pride and Prejudice*. I expected to find a familiar story and a moment of escape, yet I found peace and rest instead. I discovered sanctuary in Jane's witty repartee, stability in a world confined to a drawing room – despite being much broader – and a rhythm to both life and language that felt grounded and flowed languidly.

As I moved through Jane's six completed novels, I also found friends. Charlotte Lucas understood my uncertainty and anxiety when pondering the future as she sought to achieve her own security through marriage with Mr Collins. Anne Elliot sympathized with my loss and pain as Captain Wentworth returned to the county – visiting his sister at Kellynch Hall – and ignored and slighted her. Jane Bennet offered a model of thoughtful tranquility in difficult circumstances as she reconciled herself to Mr Bingley's silent and sudden departure for London, with the only explanation coming from the hand of his manipulative sister. Elinor Dashwood taught me how to hold it together when everything felt like it was falling apart, as she guided her family through a move from Norland Park, her sister through heartbreak and illness, and her broken heart when Lucy told her of her own engagement to Edward.

Elizabeth Bennet, of course, gave what she gives best – sparkle. I definitely needed that. Her confidence and wit buoyed me and gave me hope, as did her humility. She was willing to reassess her opinions and to see things – life, her family, Mr Darcy – from a different perspective – all while stealing our hearts, along with Mr Darcy's, with her "fine eyes" and "lively, playful disposition." Even young Catherine Morland brought something to the table. She taught me to look around, to not take things for granted, and to be grateful no matter what the future might hold. Yes, Jane Austen's stories gave me solace and her characters became friends. Then she gave me a new career…

Prior to my injury I had worked in marketing. Once upon a time I hoped I might write, but I always believed I would write nonfiction, perhaps even return to graduate school and become a teacher. While I loved to read fiction, writing it was not something I considered, nor did I find it intriguing. Yet, during my second reading of *Pride and Prejudice*, a character

My Good Friend Jane

emerged within my imagination. She was young, like so many of Jane's heroines, and she stood at her first significant coming-of-age moment – and her world was not Regency England, as many homages to Austen are set within. She did not don an empire-line dress nor did she walk long in the shrubbery. She was scrappy, angry, hurt, and living and striving – definitely not thriving – in today's world, struggling with the pressures of her times, as did Jane's heroines when she penned them onto slips of paper in her drawing room.

This character's name was Samantha Moore. She was unexpected and I wasn't quite sure what to do with her. But as I read on, she continued to take shape. Her voice emerged, as did her pain and anger, as well as her self-defense mechanism. Growing up in Chicago's foster care system, Sam's childhood was full of trauma and she grew to protect herself by hiding behind the personas of her favourite fictional characters. If someone asked what she thought, she might reply in the words of Charlotte Lucas rather than subject her own opinions, and her own vulnerability, to examination or ridicule.

She even "told" me how it all began for her, and that story made it into the final manuscript:

"I thought about you last night and stayed up reading *Emma*. I adore her, though she's out of my reach. Can you imagine such confidence and assurance of your own significance? Do you know anyone who would dare declare that he or she "could not change for the better"? I'd like to believe that – even for a moment.

But no, I gravitate toward Fanny Price, morally spot-on but commonly thought dull. Or Anne Elliot, demure and kind, not one to stand out in a crowd. Or the ever-practical and sensible Charlotte Lucas. Those dear friends I understand. I found my first copy of *Pride and Prejudice* on the "L"[1] when I was nine. I loved Austen's world. It was safe

---
1 The L refers to Chicago's elevated rapid transit train system.

and I could breathe. By the time I looked up, the book was disintegrating from wear and tear and I had barely registered two foster placement switches..."

Yes, Jane Austen's characters gave me one of my own and she grew in so many similar ways – in perception (Elizabeth), humility (Emma), awareness (Catherine), moderation (Marianne), and emotional honesty (Elinor). Yet, Samantha needed something more. She needed to eventually lay down all those characters, all those fictional journeys which provided safety, and discover her own voice, along with the courage and vulnerability to use it. For that I got a little help from another writer. Jean Webster's 1911 classic *Daddy Long Legs* provided the framework and epistolary structure, along with the idea of "hiding" Samantha's story on two levels – she was a woman hiding within characters and her story was enfolded within the framework of another. Four years later, this character and idea became my debut novel, *Dear Mr. Knightley*.

And if you're wondering how the title came about, Sam "told" me that too...:

"If you are truly a "Mr. Knightley," I can do this. I can write these letters. I trust you chose that name as a reflection of your own character. George Knightley is a good and honourable man – even better than Fitzwilliam Darcy, and few women put anyone above Mr Darcy.

Yes, Darcy's got the tempestuous masculinity and brooding good looks, but Knightley is a kinder, softer man with no pretence or dissimilation. He's a gentleman. And I can write with candour to a silent gentlemen, and I can believe he will not violate this trust."

While I never "hid" a character with Jane again in such an overt manner, I returned to her books as a touchpoint and the basis for the common language we booklovers speak in both *Lizzy & Jane* and *The Austen Escape*. And, though I've moved onto spies, forgers, and other nefarious individuals in

My Good Friend Jane

my novels, Jane Austen continues to guide how I think and how I write. And I'm not alone. She remains one of the most enduring influences on novelists today and that's a remarkable feat. Yet, it's perfectly understandable as well. After all, Jane Austen accomplished something with brilliance we novelists hope to achieve with a modicum of success every time we create a new story: She accurately, decisively, and with great wit splayed the reality and entirety of human nature before us – all our foibles, conundrums, and defeats, all our sacrifices, glory, and deepest desires. And that, my dear friends, hasn't changed in 250 years.

Happy Birthday, Jane!

Katherine Reay is a national bestselling and award-winning author of twelve novels and one non-fiction work. A Phi Beta Kappa graduate of Northwestern University, her writing has appeared in numerous publications, including *Redbook, USA TODAY, The Daily Beast, Criminal Element,* and many more. She holds a master's in marketing from Northwestern University and is a co-founder and host of the What the Dickens Book Club on Facebook and The 10 Minute Book Talk on Instagram. Katherine resides in Montana with her husband and their dogs. Her latest novel, *The English Masterpiece* centres upon a forged Picasso found in the Tate Gallery in 1973 London.

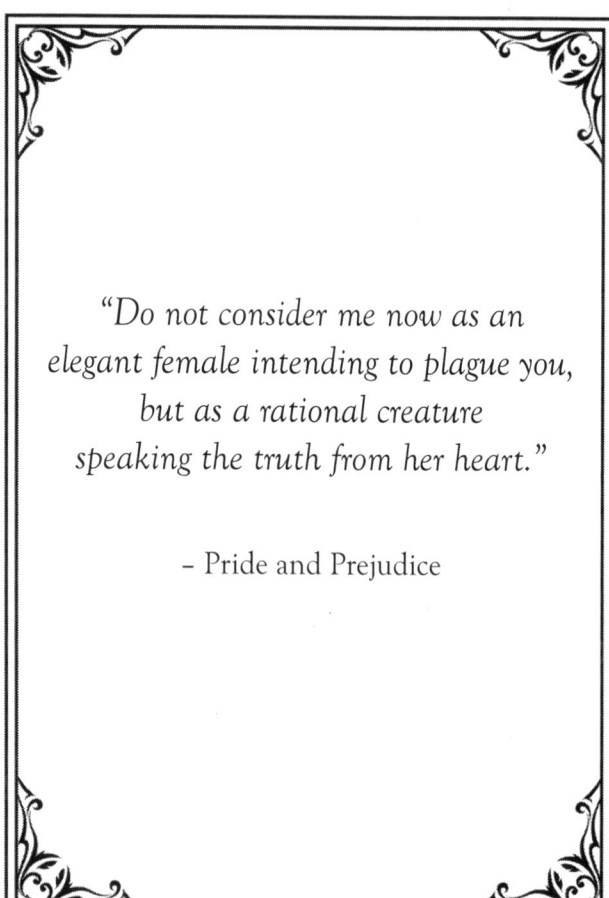

"Do not consider me now as an elegant female intending to plague you, but as a rational creature speaking the truth from her heart."

– Pride and Prejudice

"Mrs Long told me last night that he sat close to her for half an hour without once opening his lips."

Charlotte

Talulah Riley

It is a fact that gets repeated so often it becomes a truism – a factoid if you will, or fake news – that no female friendship exists without an element of rivalry. I pick my way carefully along the edges of this thought as I wait for Lizzie. She's already fifteen minutes late to the overpriced wine-bar (her suggestion) that I know to be an approximately three-minute Uber ride from her flat.

I had arrived exactly on time, of course. I allotted a generous twenty minutes to drive to the station and find a parking space. Then there was the twenty-six-minute train ride from Watford Junction to Euston. Three stops on the Northern Line and one on Piccadilly took me the best part of half-an-hour. And then I walked for five drizzly minutes in my old suede pumps.

Rivalry implies an element of competition, but our paths diverged dramatically and so long ago. Surely, we're playing entirely different games now. Yet still, she makes me wait.

Perhaps she just needs to be sure of my undivided attention for her entrance. Lizzie always does everything so perfectly, so deliberately, that she can't bear to have any of her actions unobserved, even something as pedestrian as walking into a restaurant, a trait that speaks to a kind of insecurity. Although she'd laugh in my face if I dared to describe her as insecure. Okay, she doesn't do all things perfectly – nothing that would require too much effort on her part – but the normal stuff, like walking and talking, that most people just get on with, it's here that she tries to distinguish herself.

I think about picking up my phone and texting Bill,

Charlotte

checking on the kids, just so that I'm not looking for her as she arrives. But no, this is my oldest and dearest friend – if she needs the security of my approbation, then I am very happy to give it to her. I sip my wine and watch the door.

I see her through the glass front of the bar striding along the pavement – she always was an excellent walker – moving easily in flats, what need has she for extra height? I am a keen observer as Lizzie chats easily with the maître d', she scans the room and spots me at my table, her face breaking into a smile as she points me out. I feel my own face stretching wide in response and wonder why smiling feels so strange to me. I think about what my face must look like to her, despairing that my natural reaction might somehow seem like it must be a studied gesture.

Lizzie was beautiful enough that she could've been in the 'cool group' at school. The reason we became friends instead was because she just didn't care about cool. Lizzie was clever. And funny. Really funny. We shared a dark sense of humour. As teenagers we would gossip and laugh – an odd pairing, from an outsider's perspective – but at that age we were entirely aligned.

'Sorry, sorry,' she says, throwing her arms around me, 'Things have been crazy.' I accept this as an excuse for her lateness, even though Lizzie has no husband, no children, no pets, no claims on her after-work hours. She pulls back to look at me, taking my face tenderly in both her hands. 'It's so good to see you,' she continues, 'God, I've missed you.' Her fine eyes search mine as if asking an unspoken question. I realise this is probably the most aimable physical contact I've had with another human being since the last time I saw her, three months ago. 'How are you? How's Bill? How're the kids?' she fires off, as she removes her coat and sits down.

'Oh gosh, have some wine first,' I say, summoning a waiter, knowing that she doesn't really care to hear about my family.

Encounters with Jane Austen

She can't help but flirt with the waiter. She flirts with everyone. They all do, the Bennet women. Lizzie is particularly skilled. She has an elbows-out, chin-up, take-it-or-leave-it approach that most people find irresistible. The waiter is not immune. He promises her tastes of three different bottles. She makes such a show, deliberating between the three, that I want to scream. She swirls the glasses, seductively describes the legs and the nose ('stop anthropomorphising fermented grapes!' I think), says something coy in clumsy, school-girl French. Finally, she has her choice, and our conversation turns immediately, inevitably, to her love life.

Here, I have lived vicariously for many years. Her fantasies have been my fantasies. Initially, Lizzie seemed like the winner in this regard – countless admirers, glamorous adventures, incredible freedom, romantic exploration – but the older we get (and we are getting old, much as she tries to deny it), the more obvious it is that my way is the better way. We argued about it once, our differing views of a woman's agency in love. She was shocked when I married Bill Collins, a friend of hers from university who had been slavishly devoted to her all through their time there. She couldn't understand why I would want her cast-off, why I would want Bill at all – she didn't think he was good enough for me.

Lizzie was, and is, a hopeless romantic. And by that, I mean she is a fantasist: a woman with romantic ideas so detached from the reality of life that she might as well have been born ugly. All the male characters Lizzie finds most attractive are fictional. And they're written by women.

Amazing, I think, *how such an intelligent woman can be so obtuse.*

Despite her experience, her body count far exceeding mine, she still has absolutely no idea what a man is. 'James and I broke up,' she declares, with a dramatic sigh.

'Oh no! What happened?'

'You mean what happened this time,' she says, with a sly

Charlotte

smile, 'You must be so sick of my craziness, Charlotte. I can feel your disapproval.'

'I just want you to be happy. Can't you fix things, with James?'

'He gives me the ick. Besides, the onus is on him to get back in touch with me. No way am I going to be the one to reach out first.'

Heaven forbid, Lizzie Bennet should have to dismount from her high horse. Lizzie is a product of our times; she has been taught by society to expect the impossible in all things. She is so manipulated and constrained by the norms of our day that she truly believes a woman can 'have it all.' Her level of entitlement astonishes me – she thinks a man should not only be physically attractive, with an interesting, creative and high-paying job, but that he should be morally superior, funny, easy-going and open-minded (free of bigotry and prejudice), unusually intelligent, a great cook, handy around the home, brilliant in bed, a skilled conversationalist, sensitive to her monthly cycle, playful, romantic, share her hobbies and her politics, oh, and he has to want kids and be prepared to be a hands-on father whilst maintaining the above. And that's before she gets into the weird specifics, the things that give her the ick: 'I don't like guys who wear chinos,' or 'I could never date someone who listens to podcasts while he runs.' Lizzie gives her opinion very decidedly, as if she is the ultimate authority. What she is willing to give and sacrifice to such a man in return is never the subject of our discussions, funnily enough. In fact, I've heard her say, 'If I could fall for a man who would love me enough, exactly as I am, see the real me, accept all my quirks and failures, then I would be very well pleased.'

Amazing, I think, *how such an intelligent woman can be so obtuse.*

I see so many of our contemporaries suffering from a similar delusion. I pity them.

Encounters with Jane Austen

She gets drunk quickly, this evening. Not more than half-an-hour into sitting down and she is scrolling Instagram, looking at pictures of Fitz Darcy and his wife, Caro. We don't usually mention Mr Darcy.

'Ugh, look at them snuggled up at some Scottish hunting lodge,' she groans.

'What are they hunting?' I ask with a grin, trying to lighten the mood, but she ignores my question.

'Why? Why?' she asks.

I assume she is asking, 'Why isn't it me snuggled up with Fitz at a Scottish hunting lodge, instead of getting drunk here with you?' and decide her question is rhetorical. Besides, I don't think she'd care to hear my answer: because when you get a chance with a man as sweet-but-spectrumy as Fitz Darcy you don't go and flirt outrageously with his hot-but-psychopathic corporate nemesis. George Wickham, another of her disastrous conquests. We don't usually mention him, either.

Just as we're nearing the end of our time together, she reaches across the table for my hand, 'No, really,' she slurs, 'How is Bill? How're you guys doing?'

'Same old, same old,' I trill, 'Just both very busy. Catherine keeps him running all hours, day and night.'

Lizzie snorts and rolls her eyes. Catherine is Bill's boss, and he worships her. The woman has no sense of boundaries, my husband is an easy target. She imposes endless tasks and requests; weekends, late nights, bank holidays, Catherine comes first.

'Fine by me,' I say wryly, 'I'm so caught up with the kids, you know, and the house…'

Lizzie kisses my hand. 'Do you know, Charlotte, I do believe I envy you.' She smiles, sweetly and sincerely, and I can feel the blush creeping up my neck. Finally. Finally, she admits that I was right. Lizzie had been quite cruel in her reaction when I married

Charlotte

Bill, all those years ago, but now she sees I am vindicated.

'I'm such a mess,' she says, giggling, 'Selfish. Lonely. Going to die an old maid. Oh, Charlotte, can you forgive me?'

One of Lizzie's best qualities is her ability to laugh at herself. She has a talent for finding humour in the direst situations. 'There's nothing to forgive,' I say, gently, 'Nothing at all.'

We part on the pavement outside the restaurant, with a big hug. Lizzie is very good at hugs, she puts her whole body and heart into them, and I feel literally enveloped in the warmth of her friendship. I love her, I do.

As she slips elegantly into her cab, I take out my phone and text Bill:

Just headed home now, darling.

He responds almost immediately:

Okay, my dear. Children asleep and we're all fine here. Hope you've had a good evening.

On the train ride home, I am filled with an unusual rush of affection for my husband. There are few moments in my marriage that have caused me any real joy, but I think that this absolute contentment with my lot, Lizzie's absolution, has brought me a feeling of happiness so profoundly comforting that I am awed by it. Bill is not a handsome man, he's not particularly smart or amusing, he is, in fact, pompous and often ridiculous. I wasn't unaware of his defects when I married him, which I think Lizzie thought was the case – it was the fact that I married him anyway, despite his faults: that is what love is. It's a pragmatic choice. The reality of marriage to a man – it's not an escape route to a fantasy happy-ever-after, quite the opposite – it's a continual choice to put your own needs second

Encounters with Jane Austen

to that of the relationship. A harsh reality that most women are unable to face up to. Lizzie, for example, does not have the level of discipline or self-sacrifice needed to maintain a long-term relationship. My life is spent in service to my husband and children, and in return I get the stability of a comfortable home and the security of a man who is not abusive, suffers no addictions and is not adulterous. An ordinary man for an ordinary woman – I have no delusions of grandeur – and my idea of perfect love. Love is duty, duty is love, and there is no duty without obligation. I have the freedom to pursue my own interests, once I have discharged my daily commitments at home. I am never lonely. I am needed. I have purpose. I created life.

Safety and familiarity, I think, opening the front door to our home to be greeted by the dog, who raises himself carefully from his basket and approaches sleepily, his tail wagging gently. I pat his head, listening to the soft sounds of the television from the living room.

Bill is there, stretched out asleep and snoring on the sofa. He is, objectively, a quite unattractive prospect, particularly when unconscious and drooling – but so much the safer for it. I find his clumsy physicality supremely comforting. Suddenly becoming aware of my presence, he startles awake. 'Oh, my dear, you're home,' he says, his greeting so similar in style to the dog that I almost want to pat him on the head. 'Did you ladies have fun?'

'You know Lizzie,' I say, 'Another man crisis.'

'A shame,' he says, shaking his head, 'But not unexpected.'

He jumps as his phone buzzes with a text message, and he reaches for it urgently, scanning the screen with a frown.

'Catherine?' I guess, pleasantly. He is so absorbed he no longer acknowledges me. I go upstairs to check on the children, both peaceful in slumber. Bill comes first, his work comes first, Catherine comes first.

Charlotte

By the time I come back down, Bill is snoring again. The poor man does work hard. I switch off the television, pick up the empty whiskey tumbler and go to shake him awake. Before I can, his phone buzzes with a text notification. I glance at the screen: not Catherine, but Lizzie.

I take my own phone from my pocket, to see if Lizzie is trying to urgently get hold of me, but no messages. Bill snores on.

I pick up his phone. The message is one word from Lizzie:

pervert

I click through to their text thread, scroll backwards through the exchange:

i'll think of you when I do
give her a kiss from me
got it
she's on her way back to you now
you ladies play nice now 😉
can't wait – just about to meet C now. i'd rather be seeing you than your wife
you get to see all of me next week
fuck, i miss you. i need you now. 🍆

Carefully, so carefully, I replace my husband's phone on the sofa armrest. I didn't know my husband knew the meaning of the aubergine emoji. The emoji use seems important somehow. The Bill Collins I know doesn't use emojis. He speaks in full sentences. He is an overly formal man.

I take the whiskey glass through to the kitchen and place it quietly in the sink. Slowly, I climb the stairs to my marital bed.

Amazing, I think, *how such an intelligent woman can be so obtuse.*

Encounters with Jane Austen

Talulah Riley is an English actress and novelist. She played Mary Bennet in the 2005 film *Pride and Prejudice,* and is known for her roles in film and television, including *St. Trinians, The Boat that Rocked, Inception, Dr Who,* and the HBO series *Westworld*. Her two novels, *Acts of Love* and *The Quickening* are published by Hodder and Stoughton.

"Our scars make us know that
our past was for real."

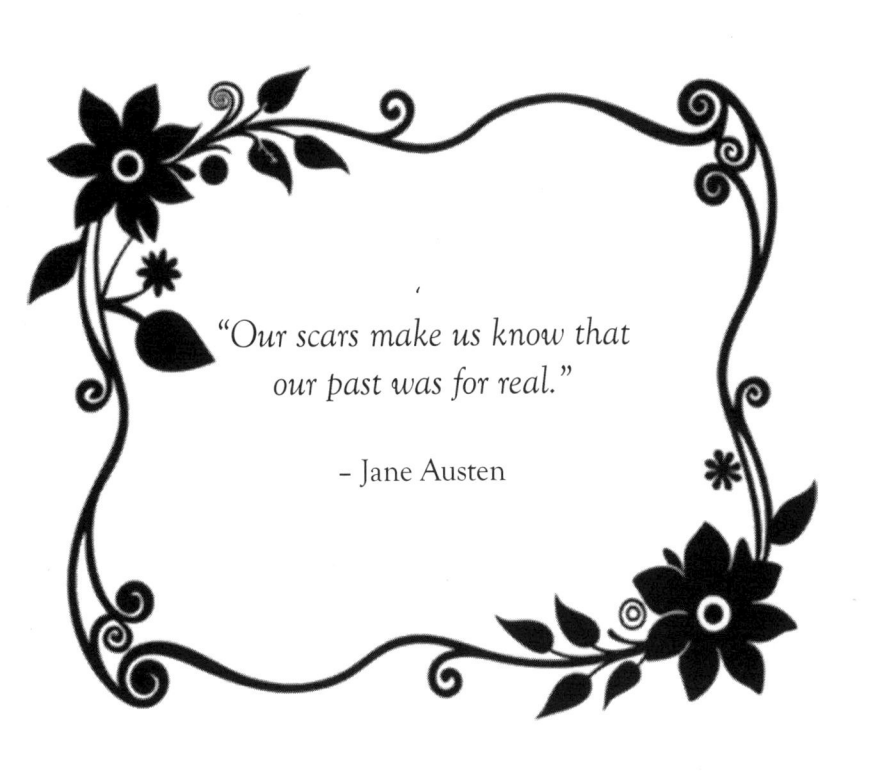

– Jane Austen

She saw herself seated beneath a tent, tenderly flirting with at least six officers at once.

How to find a Partner in Oxford

Kimberley Bailey

Move to another city

Live in Oxford, Illinois

Arrive in Oxford with a partner

Include London in your dating range

Pretend your age is not 32 but don't lie

See if you can hang out with DPhil students while wearing bright clothing, seeming young at heart

Ask a friend from back home if they'll marry you if you're still single in five years' time

Go on many dates, it's a numbers game!

Then ditch the numbers game strategy

And take up many hobbies, but don't speak to anyone when you arrive

Work on your opening lines and then realise you're fine at meeting people – it's the deciding to date them part that you need to practise

Convince yourself to go on second dates

And then make it harder for yourself to say sorry it's not you it's me, because now you've committed to a second date

Take up writing poetry about how bad you are at dating

And then read it at an open mic night

Encounters with Jane Austen

Convince yourself that it's better to find partners in your 30s anyways because you know who you are

Realise you know too much

Try and bury some of those gems you've learnt about yourself over the years

Think about messaging all your exes to fill in a feedback form; iteration is the new numbers game

See if you can salvage the end of this poem with something humorous

Regret saying humour because you might have to live up to that now

Realise you've given no one advice and then relax because no-one wants advice from a stranger anyways

Go back to matching with people on Bumble that you never msg

Try again to land your poem

Realise it might just have to be the same way you end all the dates that aren't going well

Stay for too long and then make it seem like you were having a lovely time

Kimberley lives and works in Oxford. She was inspired to begin writing poetry by David Whyte on the On Being podcast. Her poems are often written for specific occasions, celebrating a friend's birthday or to be read aloud at a colleague's farewell. She's enjoying finding playfulness in her poetry and hopes to always find a home in this practice.

"*Every man is surrounded by a neighborhood of voluntary spies.*"

– Jane Austen

The officers of the —shire

A Role Model for Women's Solidarity[1]

Emily Midorikawa & Emma Claire Sweeney

In 1815, Jane Austen had a decision to make. The agreement she had negotiated with John Murray entitled her to twelve presentation copies of *Emma,* the fourth of her novels to be published. After fulfilling obligations to relatives, she had been left with only three remaining copies. These, she earmarked for wildly different recipients: an amateur-writer friend, Anne Sharp; the bestselling novelist, Maria Edgeworth; and the Prince Regent to whom the novel had been dedicated – at his behest.

The stories behind Austen's choice of these three recipients reveal moral dilemmas that still speak with uncanny resonance to women today.

Austen had long despised the Prince Regent for his famed womanizing. A few years earlier, when a royal sex scandal had swept the nation, her sympathies had rested with his estranged wife. 'Because she is a woman,' the novelist explained privately to a female friend, '& because I hate her Husband.'

But then, as now, it was dangerous to stand up publicly to a powerful man – especially once he had set his sights on you. On receiving a royal invitation to visit one of the prince's residences, Austen had essentially been duty-bound to attend. It was in these lavishly decorated chambers, heavy on crystal and gilt, that she had been invited to dedicate *Emma* to His Royal Highness.

---

[1] This essay was first published in *The Washington Post* on December 14th 2017.

Encounters with Jane Austen

Austen must have abhorred the prospect of associating herself with someone she considered a philanderer who flaunted his wealth when most of the country was struggling to make ends meet. The week after her visit, Austen had written to the court librarian, daring to ask whether she might avoid making the requested dedication. Since the librarian's response had failed to offer reassurance, Austen concluded that she could not risk spurning the ruler of the land.

In any case, she could console herself that such a dedication might help her leverage greater financial security and literary acclaim — aims she was not shy to admit. And she could at least reserve her final copies of *Emma* for two fellow female writers, although her reasons for choosing each of them could not have been more different.

Maria Edgeworth, then one of Britain's most famous novelists, was far better known than Austen herself. A resulting endorsement from this established author could have brought Austen improved sales and greater recognition. But Edgeworth failed even to acknowledge receipt of the gift. She would later privately confess to admiring Austen's final novel, *Persuasion*, but — perhaps protecting her space at the top — she never openly praised her literary peer.

In contrast, Austen's response to the work of her contemporary offers inspiration to ambitious women today. Using one of the few outlets available to her, she publicly complimented Edgeworth's work within the pages of one of her own novels, *Northanger Abbey*. This sisterly act continues to draw attention to Edgeworth now that Austen's fame far outshines the author she so admired. Such is the importance of talented women amplifying each other's achievements.

Austen's conduct feels particularly relevant during our current era in which women so often work together to try to overturn the kind of threatening behaviour that still too often prevails among powerful men. The little-known story

A Role Model for Women's Solidarity

behind Austen's class-defying friendship with Anne Sharp – an amateur playwright who'd worked as one of the family's governesses – suggests that these two women understood the importance of female solidarity in the face of male entitlement. By selecting Sharp as the final recipient of a precious copy of *Emma*, Austen chose to favour this unlikely friend over remaining family members including one of her brothers, Sharp's former employer.

By this stage, Sharp had confided in Austen about the trials she had endured over the course of her working life. In one home, she had suffered the advances of a man who held power over her – a common problem for governesses, who, as neither typical servants nor family members, were vulnerable to predatory upper-class men. Austen, long aware of her friend's isolation, had always gone out of her way to help. She not only provided a shoulder to cry on, she also offered more practical help: arranging on a number of occasions for Sharp to stay with her and her female relatives, and even looking for alternative employment for Sharp. Most importantly, perhaps, Austen accepted without question the governess's allegations of sexual harassment.

Sharp would have made a far more fitting dedicatee for *Emma* than the licentious Prince Regent. Sharp would have understood the predicament of the heroine, who finds herself trapped in a carriage with a man who repeatedly takes hold of her against her will. When he ignores her quiet attempts to rebut his advances, Emma summons the courage to speak – her voice a gift of resistance to those women who experience such struggles today and those of us who dare to stand with them.

Encounters with Jane Austen

Emily Midorikawa is the author of two nonfiction books: *Out of the Shadows: Six Visionary Victorian Women in Search of a Public Voice* and *A Secret Sisterhood: The Literary Friendships of Jane Austen, Charlotte Brontë, George Eliot and Virginia Woolf* (co-written with Emma Claire Sweeney, and with a foreword by Margaret Atwood). She is a winner of the Lucy Cavendish Fiction Prize. Her debut novel, *A Tiny Speck of Black and then Nothing*, will be published in 2026.

Emma Claire Sweeney is the author of a novel, *Owl Song at Dawn,* which won Nudge Book of the Year (literary category) and a nonfiction book, *A Secret Sisterhood: The literary friendships of Jane Austen, Charlotte Brontë, George Eliot and Virgina Woolf* (co-written with Emily Midorikawa, and with a foreword by Margaret Atwood). Emma has won Society of Authors, Arts Council and Royal Literary Fund awards.

She

Zita Holbourne

She

Navigates sexism and misogyny
Lives under the shadow of patriarchy
Expected to obey and be submissive
Knowing to survive she must be assertive

Branded as far too forward when she speaks out
Told it's not ladylike when 'girls' like her SHOUT!
Expected to obey and do as she's told
For standing her ground, she's aggressively trolled

Breaks through glass ceilings but told to know her place
Branded troublemaker when she takes up space
Judged on how she looks instead of what she does
Won't be silenced, so told she's making a fuss

On buses and trains forced to fight manspreading
Mother of three but childbirth needs mansplaining?
Stands up for her rights but labelled "drama queen"
Abused and bullied for daring to be seen

Encounters with Jane Austen

Nights out – sexually harassed and body shamed
But when she takes action against this, she's blamed
Expected to be a housewife and mother
And between the sheets be a red-hot lover

Still, she goes out to work to earn a living
Then takes on all her family's care giving
When it gets too much she acts like nothing's wrong
Keeps everyone else going, always stays strong

Valued for appearance but not attributes
Pressured to accept outdated attitudes
Demeaned for rejecting manipulation
Gaslit for challenging discrimination

This isn't the eighteenth or nineteenth century
Women live and succeed independently
She will not be forced to comply or conform
She's creating her own destiny and norm

If he wishes to earn her respect and love
He must hear her speak truth of the heart here of
Don't consider her an elegant female
An irrational creature, fragile and frail

Intending to plague with femininity
But a woman with whom he has affinity
Respect and celebration won't go amiss
Or liberation from pride and prejudice

She

Treat her with love, friendship and humanity
With her, act with sense and sensibility
If she's to love him, he can't be chauvinist
If he truly loves her, be a feminist

Zita Holbourne FRSA is a multi–award winning, multidisciplinary artist, author, educator, community activist, equality and human rights campaigner and trade union leader. Her creative practice focuses on equality, freedom, justice and rights and includes work as a visual artist, performance poet, writer and vocalist. She is the author of the book of poetry, *Striving for Equality Freedom and Justice,* co-author of *Roots and Rebellion*, winner of the Jessica Kingsley Writing Prize and featured in the award-winning book, *Here We Stand, Women Changing the World* and recently *Encounters with James Baldwin* (2024) published by Supernova Books.

Zita is the co-founder and National Chair of Black Activists Rising Against Cuts (BARAC) UK, National Co-Chair of Artists' Union England. She is, a fellow of the Royal Society of Arts and an Honorary Fellow of the University of Wales Trinity Saint David. Awards include: Global Diversity List 100, Caribbean Global Awards – Outstanding Global Arts and Culture and Best Global Community Influencer, Legacy Lifetime Achievement Award for Equality Champion, Olive Morris Award, Ethnicity Awards top 100.

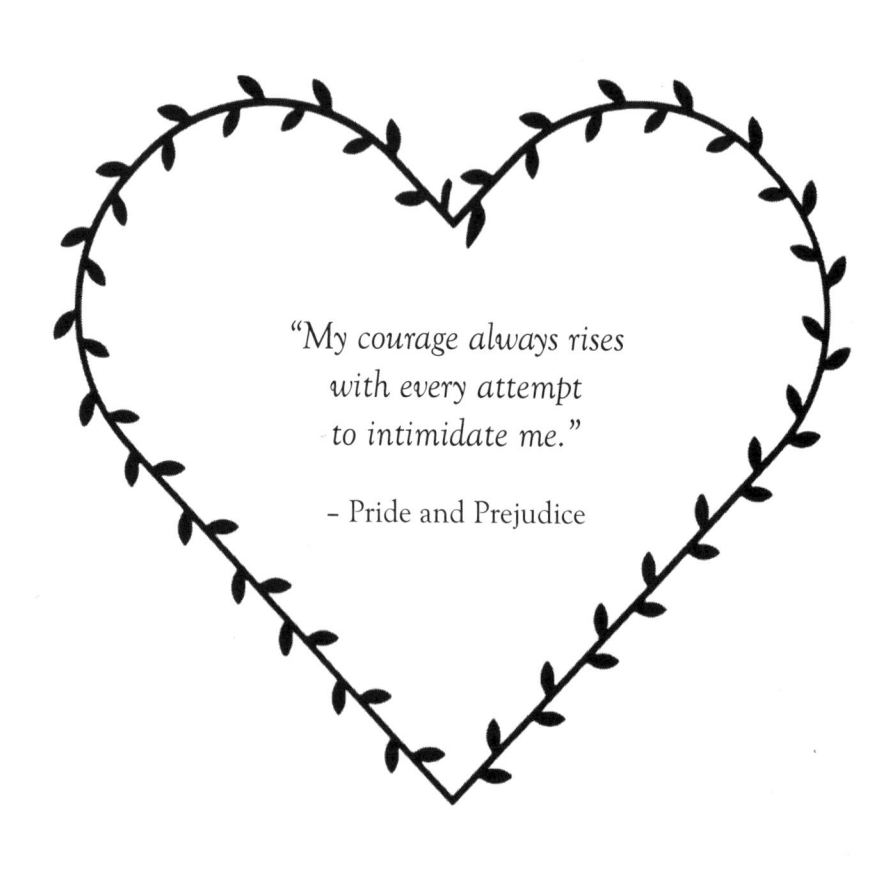

*"My courage always rises
with every attempt
to intimidate me."*

– Pride and Prejudice

They had forgotten to leave any message for
the ladies of Rosings.

Georgiana Darcy – Pistols at Dawn

Julia Miller

"Torrential rain lashed the castle, thunder rolled around the sodden heath, and jagged flashes of lightning illuminated the awful scene. Two pistols blazed, and two bodies fell dead upon the sward. It was a sight too horrible to behold."

I closed *The Castle of Wolfersdorf* and sighed with satisfaction. Now I knew how to avenge myself on Mr Wickham.

*

It is a fact known only to my closest family, that when I was fifteen years old, I intended to elope with George Wickham. I do not understand how he bewitched me, but I was very young and he was very handsome. I was on holiday in Ramsgate with my cousin, Anne de Bourgh, attended by my companion, Mrs Younge. It was only my brother Fitzwilliam's arrival that prevented the elopement and saved me from certain disgrace.

I was not close to Anne then. Our mothers had intended her to marry Fitzwilliam, but she and I had little in common. My brother, too, was indifferent to her, as he was to the other main contender for his heart – Caroline Bingley.

I spent many evenings laughing in private at Miss Bingley's obvious attempts at intimacy and Fitzwilliam's equally obvious disdain. He thought his exchanges with her unobserved, but he was mistaken. My quiet appearance harbours a keen appreciation for life's absurdities, and my apparent shyness does not prevent me noticing and smiling at the foibles of those around me. I did

Georgiana Darcy – Pistols at Dawn

not know if this were a family characteristic, as my parents were no longer alive, but I was delighted to discover I shared this trait with my dear sister-in-law.

Lizzy's entrance to our household furnished me with all I hoped to find in a sister. She was more open than I in her merriment, and dearly loved to laugh. More important still, she showed me how to be brave, and though I was still in awe of my brother, I came to take greater liberties with him and to be less fearful of other men.

Accordingly, I was determined to show Mr Wickham I was no longer subject to his influence and would endeavour to prevent other young ladies falling under his spell. I vowed to take vengeance on his attempt to ruin my character.

The means of revenge presented itself to me during a visit to Rosings. As Anne and I finished *The Castle of Wolfersdorf*, I looked idly up at the library wall and counted no less than seventeen flintlocks. One was shinier than the rest. I took it down, and the weight of the gun gave me a feeling of power.

'That is a fearsome instrument,' said Anne. 'Do you have an idea for its use?'

I was surprised at her forthrightness. Like myself, she is somewhat reserved, and though we had been much thrown together in the past, we had seldom found two words to exchange with each other. Now, however, we had discovered a mutual love of horrid tales and had taken to sharing our novel reading together.

'I think I may have a use for it,' I replied. 'Can you shoot?'

'I never tried. But I should like to. And you?'

'I should very much like to learn. But do you know where there are bullets?'

We rummaged among the drawers in the library and found a small leather box at the back of the writing desk. Inside were several dozen lead bullets. I dropped one down the barrel of the pistol, conjuring for myself an image of how this might be used to effect.

'It wants gunpowder,' said Anne.

We searched eagerly in the depths of drawers and cupboards, and behind the books on the shelves, and at length we unearthed a metal canister filled with a dark grey powder.

'And see here!' exclaimed Anne. 'This is a book educating officers in the use of muskets.'

That afternoon, Anne and I retreated to a secluded part of the woods. First, we learned how gunpowder is used to create the spark that fires the bullets. Understanding now how dangerous gunpowder could be, we placed our metal canister among the tree roots for safety.

We were still reading the instruction book when we heard someone whistling close by and discerned the steady tramp of boots approaching through the wet leaves. It was Tom, the stable-boy from Rosings. We regarded him warily, but he smiled and held out some little paper rolls to us, indicating we should join him in smoking what I took to be tobacco.

The forwardness of his invitation thrilled rather than shocked us, but, fearful of igniting the gunpowder, we endeavoured to draw him away from the tree. He laughed at our supposed timidity and would not follow, so we thanked him for his offer and quitted the spot, warning him that this was not a good place to linger.

We had reached the ha-ha when we heard a small explosion and saw a little plume of dark smoke rising above the wood. This was followed by loud cursing, and a moment later Tom came into view, his face blackened with soot. He ran across the field and disappeared.

I looked at Anne. She looked at me. Tom was unhurt, and our relief gave way to laughter. But now we had no gunpowder.

Georgiana Darcy – Pistols at Dawn

*

The next day, we returned to our book, and learned we needed saltpetre, charcoal and sulphur to make the black powder. There was a small amount of charcoal in the medicine cabinet, where it was kept as a treatment for indigestion. We tipped it into an empty perfume bottle and hid it in the stables.

I despaired of finding saltpetre, but Anne had overheard the staff talk of its use for cooling wine, and so we braved the depths of the cellar. The shadowy corners and moist stone ledges lent an air of romance which banished our timidity. Anne held the lamp, and we searched in every cranny, but when we found the saltpetre barrel, alas, it was empty.

We were close to the exit when the cellar door creaked, and, fearing discovery, we extinguished our lamp and hid behind a cask. Heavy boots descended, followed by a lighter step, and we heard hushed voices.

'Really, Mellors, I cannot think why you wanted to come down here.'

'It's somewhere different, Your Ladyship. Adds a bit of spice to the encounter, don't it?'

They passed us and continued to the darker reaches of the cellar. Anne took my arm, and we fled up the stairs, illuminated only by the light from the half-opened doorway. Once in my apartment, I was surprised to see Anne shaking with laughter.

'I had heard a rumour of my mother's behaviour, and now I have further evidence.'

'Her behaviour?'

Anne told me of the time when Mr Collins became rector of Rosings and Lady Catherine had pursued his rival candidate with amorous intent. I was all astonishment, yet somehow relieved. The lot of a single woman might not be as dull as I had feared.

Our journey into the cellar having proved fruitless, we were still in need of saltpetre.

'And sulphur,' said Anne. 'I was once dosed with elixir of vitriol to settle my weak stomach. It was the most unpleasant treatment I ever underwent. I took one small sip and poured the remainder onto the plants. They died, as I'm sure I should have done, had I drunk it.'

'Then where shall we find any?' I asked.

'There is none in the medicine cabinet, but the apothecary will have it,' she said. 'And he will have saltpetre.'

'Will he not know what we are about, if we ask for those two items?'

Anne assured me he was accustomed to her general indisposition and would not question her. I was not so certain, but she had her ponies harnessed and we set off in the phaeton.

Unfortunately, we could not reach the village without passing Mr Collins in the churchyard. 'My dear Miss de Bourgh, Miss Darcy. I am overjoyed to see you. I trust your dear mother is well, Miss de Bourgh?'

'She is as well as she was when you last saw her, sir,' answered Anne, turning her head from him slightly.

I am sure it was not his fault, but his breath was strong, and I wondered if he too had been drinking sulphur.

'Very good, very good,' he said. 'I look forward to seeing you both at Rosings Park when I am next invited to dinner.'

We continued into the village, tethered the ponies near the village green and knocked on the door of the apothecary's house. We were ushered into the presence of a good-looking young man in a smart beige waistcoat and blue coat, whose eyes sparkled with pleasure as he looked at Anne. I was amused to see her blush and smooth a lock of hair from her forehead.

'Good day, ladies,' he said. 'I trust all is well at Rosings Park, Miss de Bourgh. How may I be of assistance?'

Georgiana Darcy – Pistols at Dawn

We had not devised an excuse for our purchases, but Anne was quick to invent one.

'Good afternoon, Mr Strickland. We come from Mr Collins. He is feeling a trifle dyspeptic, and has requested a little sulphur for his stomach.'

'Indeed,' said Mr Strickland. 'I am sorry to hear it. I will mix you a solution directly.'

'That will not be necessary, sir,' I interjected. 'The crystals will suffice.'

'Indeed,' he repeated, his eyes full of merriment. 'Is there anything else you require?'

'There is one thing,' said Anne. 'The butler is running low on saltpetre. For the wine cellar.'

'The butler?' echoed Mr Strickland. 'That is unfortunate. I would not like Lady Catherine to be lacking in chilled wine. How much would you like?'

I had not thought about the quantities, but Anne was very good at mathematics.

'Only a pound of saltpetre, I think,' she said. 'And two ounces of sulphur.'

Mr Strickland weighed the ingredients for us. 'Will that be all?'

'Yes, thank you, sir,' she replied, gazing steadily into his dark brown eyes. I nudged her and we took the parcels. It may have been my imagination, but I was sure I heard the sound of a low chuckle as we left.

We hid our packages in the stables, with the charcoal.

The next day, we prepared our powder. The kitchen staff, although surprised to see us, were occupied, and we found the necessary implements and retired to a corner.

First we ground our ingredients individually, then we boiled the saltpetre with a little water before adding the sulphur and

Encounters with Jane Austen

charcoal. We were straining the mixture through a cheesecloth when the cook appeared. He was a fearsome man, not at all intimidated by rank or power.

'Good Heaven, Miss de Bourgh, what are you doing with that black liquid?' His hands were on his hips, his moustache a-quiver. 'That is my best copper vessel.'

'I am sorry, sir,' said Anne. 'I did not know. I have not used a kitchen before.'

'That is evident,' said he. 'Does Her Ladyship know you are here?'

It is hard to speak when we are thus confronted, but I was learning to be bold.

'She does not,' I said. 'And I think it would be well if she did not know. We would not like to disturb her. And we will… we will clean the pot when we are done.'

He looked at us coldly, then departed. I was pleased to note that I was not shaking as I had been used to do.

'Come,' I said. 'We will dry the mixture in the sunshine and press it through this sieve.'

We removed to the woods and spent the afternoon preparing our powder. The final product we put in two little canisters hid in the roots of two oak trees a distance apart.

'Why do you wish to shoot?' asked Anne. 'For my part, I do not wish to kill anything. I am interested only in being a marksman, in the sport of finding my target.'

'A marksman?' I said. 'Rather, let it be a markswoman. It is not only men who can fire a pistol. But there is one man I would dearly love to shoot. Not to kill, you understand, but to hurt him. To take revenge on the harm he nearly caused me and may cause other young women.'

'How will you do this? Will you ambush him?'

'I will challenge him to a duel.'

Georgiana Darcy – Pistols at Dawn

*

The next morning, we took the shiny flintlock from the library wall and repaired to a secluded spot. There were only sixty bullets, and we must take care how we used them. We loaded the gun and I took aim at an ostrich feather from Anne's despised bandeau, tied to a low wall. I missed. Anne tried, and her bullet also went wide of its mark.

I reloaded the pistol and was about to fire again when a familiar whistling halted my action. I concealed the gun behind me as Tom the stable-boy wandered towards us.

'Morning, Miss de Bourgh. Morning, Miss Darcy.'

'Good morning, Tom.'

'Did you hear the shooters just now, miss?'

'Yes, Tom. We did.'

'You want to be careful, miss. Don't get in the way of them guns.'

'No, Tom.'

'And never load a gun you're not going to fire. You don't know who you might hit. They might be having a smoke, quiet, like, when all of a sudden this stash of gunpowder explodes. You don't want that to happen with a gun, now, do you?' He winked at us. 'Know how to shoot?'

We remained silent.

'Want me to show you?'

And so we spent the morning, and half our bullets, learning to hit a target.

*

We passed the afternoon in the library reading *The Young Man of Honour's Vade-Mecum, Being a Salutary Treatise on Duelling*. There were so many rules, I could not remember them all, but I resolved that, as the offended party, I would have the choice of weapon.

'Who will you have satisfaction with?' Anne asked me.

'His name is Wickham, and he is a scoundrel. Will you promise not to share my secret?'

'I will never tell a soul, my dear Georgiana.'

Although she had been in Ramsgate with me, she had spent the day with a friend of her mother's and had had no notion of what transpired. Now she was shocked, but fascinated.

'I had not thought your life so romantic, Georgiana. But he is a soldier. Are you not afraid he will kill you?'

'I do not think so. It seems that many men now do not aim to kill. In any case, I will wear a metal breastplate under my jacket, from the suit of armour in the gallery.'

'But what if he hit you in the arm or the leg? And duelling is not legal. If you kill Wickham, you may be executed.'

'I am not frightened,' I said. Truth be told, I was very much afraid, but I was resolved to continue. 'I have never heard of his killing anyone. And I do not intend to kill him. I only want to teach him a lesson.'

'Will he fight you if he knows your name?'

'No, I am certain even he would not fight a girl. I will call myself Edward. There are so many Edwards, he must have offended some one of them!'

We drafted a letter, and though we did not know Wickham's direction, I hoped it would reach him through my former companion, his friend Mrs Younge.

His reply came a week later, stating he was unaware of the provocation, but, as a man of honour, he was bound to accept the challenge.

I hid the letter under my pillow and hastened to tell Anne.

*

Georgiana Darcy – Pistols at Dawn

I continued to practise shooting, but shortly before the duel, I met with a fresh obstacle – we had no further bullets. This was disaster indeed.

'You are very dull, Georgiana,' said Aunt Catherine at dinner that night. 'Does she not look pale, Mr Collins?'

'I do not—' he began.

'You must take a little charcoal for your stomach, Georgiana. It is most efficacious. My men-servants are ready to accompany you and Anne to town tomorrow, but if you are indisposed, we will cancel the trip.'

'I am perfectly well, Aunt, thank you.'

'I noticed you received a letter. I hope it was not bad news from Pemberley.'

'No, Aunt. My brother and his wife are well.'

'Then there is no need to be so dispirited. I will supply all that you need for the journey.' She took a sip of wine and turned to her other guest. 'Do you require anything for your indigestion, Mr Collins? I hope you are not stinting yourself on your elixir of vitriol.'

'Indeed, Lady Catherine, I—'

'And you would do well to take some charcoal. I will have my maid fetch some from the medicine cabinet. Georgiana, pray try some of this Rhenish wine. It is quite cold. The butler has had a fresh delivery of saltpetre from Mr Strickland.'

*

The next day, I prepared for my assignation. I did not know what I should do without bullets, but I thought Wickham's team might provide the necessary ammunition. It was little enough to ask. I had specified we would have one shot each, so I would need only one bullet.

I was astonished when, on entering the library after breakfast to collect the flintlock, I saw a new leather case on the table, a row of bullets inside. I secreted both case and gun in my workbag, and hurried to the stable block.

'I hope you are right,' Anne whispered, as we set off in the coach. 'Surely Wickham will give you a bullet.'

I showed her the leather box. 'I think Tom has supplied what we need. I found this on the library table.'

She was equally amazed.

'Or perhaps your Mr Strickland anticipated our needs?' I teased her. 'He cannot have been unaware of why we wanted the sulphur and the saltpetre, and he knew there was charcoal in the cabinet.'

We spent the night at an inn next to Hampstead-heath, but I could not sleep a wink. I had not set eyes on Wickham since our planned elopement, and in the small hours of the morning, surrounded by darkness, the enormity of the step I was about to take all but overwhelmed me. I who was normally so timid, whom people regarded as shy and proud, to act in this way! I did not know where I had found this reserve of strength.

Anne felt me turning and tossing in the bed beside her, and reached out a hand to still me. 'You will have your vengeance on Wickham.'

'And if I fail to hit him?'

'You will have the satisfaction of having fought a duel and maintained your honour, even if he is unaware of your identity.'

She slept, and I lay quietly till dawn, remembering Tom's instructions and silently blessing him for giving us the bullets.

*

Two hours later, Anne and I marched boldly into the pale morning light, leaving the men-servants snoring in the inn. There was no thunder or lightning, and the grass was not sodden, merely damp with dew. Still, a faint mist rolled above

Hampstead-heath and the leaves were speckled with water droplets. It was romantic enough.

We waited impatiently until a hackney-coach drew up and Wickham alighted with two other men. One was his second, the other a physician. My adversary seemed very sure of himself, though a little taken aback to see our slight figures in the distance. We were dressed in men's garb. Anne was covered by a cloak, and I wore a mask. My hair and face were concealed, and a metal waistcoat made my body seem larger beneath its jacket.

I advanced to the chosen spot. Wickham looked at me wonderingly, but I spoke not a word. We stood back to back, and, at his second's command, each advanced eight paces. Then we turned and fired.

I do not know if he missed me by intent, but my bullet grazed the fleshy part of his thigh, low enough not to cause serious damage, but sharp enough to hurt. He gripped his leg and fell to the ground. I summoned Anne and we departed.

*

We could scarce contain ourselves on the journey home. To have avenged myself in such a way, and to have fired a true shot that hit its target, was more than I could comprehend.

'No one could accuse you of timidity now, Georgiana,' said Anne.

'No one but you knows of my actions,' I said. 'But I feel empowered. That is what matters.'

We congratulated ourselves on the success of our enterprise all the way home.

'Now,' I said, when we reached Rosings, 'we must thank Tom.'

We went to the stables, but he was not there. Mr Strickland, however, was leaving the house as we arrived. He raised his hat

Encounters with Jane Austen

and smiled broadly.

'You are returned very early, ladies. Did you not enjoy your trip to town?'

'Indeed we did enjoy it,' I replied. 'But I am surprised to see you here, sir. I hope Lady Catherine is not unwell.'

'Her Ladyship is never unwell,' said Mr Strickland. 'She summoned me to replenish her medicine cabinet and furnish a draught for Mr Collins. I was happy to supply her with more sulphur and saltpetre, and restock the powdered charcoal. Good day to you, ladies.'

He raised his hat again and continued on his way.

'He knows about the gunpowder,' said Anne. 'But no matter. It is not a crime to make it.'

'The only crime was to use it in a duel,' I said. 'And since Wickham will never tell a soul, we are safe. And here is Tom.'

The stable-boy sauntered up, smiling.

'Tom, we must thank you,' I said.

Tom was surprised. 'Thank me, miss? I was happy to help you learn to shoot.'

'Yes, of course, we are very grateful. But the ammunition. It was most kind of you to supply the extra bullets.'

He expressed amazement. 'Not me, miss. I had no bullets. I didn't know you needed 'em.'

'Not you?'

'No, miss.' And he strolled away, whistling.

'Not Tom,' said Anne. 'Then who?'

We went to the library to return the flintlock. I was just reaching up to replace it on the wall when Lady Catherine entered.

'That gun will need cleaning,' she observed. 'There are traces of powder around the barrel. And be sure to leave the remainder of the bullets in the box in the writing desk.'

Georgiana Darcy – Pistols at Dawn

She smiled briefly and swept out of the room, and I thought back over the last few weeks. The letter under my pillow … our encounter with Mr Strickland … the bullets …

*

I returned to Pemberley with many tender expressions of affection from Anne, and promises that we should meet again soon. In the meantime, we would read the latest novel, *The Abbot*, and correspond regularly about the thrilling horrors we hoped to find within its pages.

I had a new respect for my cousin and my aunt, and realised our families were united by more than the ties of blood. Anne and I had fought to overcome our timidity, each in our own way. I understood, too, that though I could never approve Lady Catherine's imperiousness, I had inherited some of the more positive aspects of her nature – a talent for observation, a strength of purpose, and a sense of humour.

Above all, I was free of the spectre of my failed elopement. I knew now, without a doubt, that my life would be what I wished it to be. I was ready for the adventure.

Julia is a lifelong fan of Jane Austen, whose work inspired her to write *Crime and Prejudice*, a collection of short stories.

Julia studied French and Spanish at Cambridge and taught English in Portugal. She later spent many happy years as a university lecturer in Australia, collecting a PhD along the way. She writes in a variety of genres, including crime and romance. All her novels contain elements of intrigue, with more than a dash of humour, and all have strong women characters.

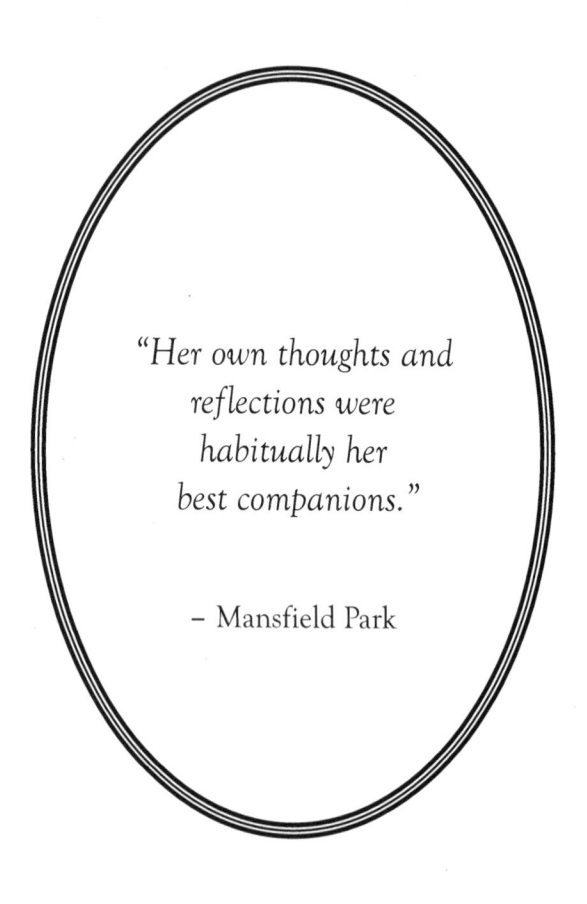

"Her own thoughts and reflections were habitually her best companions."

– Mansfield Park

"No, no; stay where you are," Elizabeth told them.

Discovering Pride in Austen's Time

Caitlin Grills

Despite being famed for some of literary history's most recognised romance stories between man and woman, Jane Austen has long been subject to interest, speculation, and excitement from the queer community. Perplexing, this may be for some, given that her novels centre upon the likes of Mr Darcy and Frederick Wentworth, welcomed into her stories for the purpose of sweeping her female protagonists off their feet and away in a wedding carriage.

But despite this, in recent years her novels have been subject to numerous retellings that seek to queer her famous love stories. Elizabeth Bennet is reimagined as a trans man, Oliver, in Gabe Cole Novoa's 2024 novel *Most Ardently: A Pride and Prejudice Remix*. Yearning to live openly with his gender expression, Oliver Bennet falls in love with Darcy while struggling against pressures to become a wife to an eligible suitor. Elizabeth Bennet is not the only character in the novel to undergo a queer transformation. Charlotte Lucas is gifted with a lesbian storyline, pursuing a relationship with a woman despite her longing to marry and settle down with a man. Additionally, in her 2020 Sapphic retelling of *Persuasion*, Amy Blythe's novel *Within my Reach* transforms an Austen classic away from its picturesque Bath setting to Auckland, New Zealand, and in doing so, swaps a quintessentially English love story for an all-female love triangle. These are just some examples in a long list of queered Austen stories.

Discovering Pride in Austen's Time

Contemporary re-writings that have become rather ubiquitous today may even be read as a continuation of the earlier performance history that saw Austen's novels adapted for the stage. Scholars such as Devoney Looser have explored the many notable examples of Victorian-era all-female casts performing stage adaptations of works such as *Pride and Prejudice*. With romance still very much – and literally – centre stage in these productions, audiences would have been witness to an early example of female drag performance. While cross-dressing was not uncommon in early theatre productions (examples include Shakespeare's *Twelfth Night*), the all-female casts of Austen stage adaptations have been subject to enquiry from academics and historians looking to uncover the queer in her ostensibly not-so queer stories and romance plots.

This active interest in finding a silver queer lining in novels that appear to remain comfortably within a heterosexual logic and timeline is perhaps inspired by the comparable nature of love as explored by Austen, and queer love, as it exists in its many shades and complexities. By loving certain people, or in certain ways, Austen's characters are often othered in return. While for Austen's characters, the risks of expressing attraction to the 'wrong' person is largely linked to 18th-century class expectations, the limitations placed on their pursuit of love, and the consequences they face if deemed to be loving inappropriately, is nonetheless comparable to those faced by queer people, then and now: judgement or disownment from one's family, societal exclusion and rejection, and being compelled to live in secrecy. It will ring true in a very particular way for many that to love and to feel loved is indeed 'to burn, to be on fire.'

Austen's protagonists do at times hover on the outskirts of the orbit that is traditional heterosexuality, while sometimes, though most often only briefly, drifting beyond it. For most, however, their fate is to be drawn swiftly back within its force through marriage. Considering this, it may be the temptation to queer heterosexual plots so culturally revered, rather than the content of the novels themselves, that inspires these modern retellings. Incidentally, it was the most notable protagonist of all – indeed, Austen herself – who successfully remained firmly outside the orbit that defines marriage and traditional heterosexual narratives. The author of some of the most famous romance stories in Britain – and beyond – remained herself unmarried, committed to a single life of prose writing. Her most intimate relationship was believed to be with her sister, Cassandra, with whom she lived until her death. The writings that contributed so immensely to the progression of the novel as a literary form are perhaps thanks to the author's apathy when faced with the potential suitors of her day and the life of servility they may so generously have offered. Thus, it may be that the urge to reimagine or construct a queerified Austen stems not so much from inside the author's novels but from without. She remained perched on the edge of traditional life, watching her characters become inevitably subsumed by its grasp.

And so, the urge to absorb Austen into the queer cultural imagination is indeed tantalising. Despite the temptation to query the sapphic tendencies of the late author, however, this must be refrained from for the sake of accuracy (the details of her sexuality have never been confirmed), and to stave off any looming accusations of appropriating Austen for the sake of the gay agenda. With this in mind, this short essay marks a disinterested attempt to place Austen's life in the context of her female contemporaries who also chose to remain unmarried and, for the most part, did so successfully. Many of the women explored here remained single in the eyes of the law for the sake of pursuing romantic – or at least, ostensibly romantic – relations with other women, but this, of course, is of mere coincidence.

A good place to begin is with perhaps the most famous lesbian – often referred to as the first modern lesbian – of

Discovering Pride in Austen's Time

Austen's time, Anne Lister (1791-1840). Born 16 years after Austen, the landowner and businesswoman recorded her many romantic and sexual escapades with women in her encrypted diaries. The code that she might have thought would be unbreakable, and indeed succeeded in concealing her elicit affairs while she was alive, enabled her to write in detail of her love for women and only women, noting once that 'a violent longing for a female companion came over me.' With a notable disregard for convention and propriety, Lister's diary also speaks much of reciprocated attractions and flirtations: 'I teazing and behaving rather amorously to her she would gladly have got into bed or done anything of the loving kind I asked her.' It was only after her death that her diaries were found in the attic of her home, Shibden Hall, and eventually de-coded by a presumably shocked and flustered John Lister, the last resident of the house.

It is perhaps unlikely that Austen's many letters, destroyed by her sister Cassandra after her death, contained quite the same content as Lister's. Nonetheless, while it took five years for Lister's private ruminations to be unveiled for the world to see, Austen's were, and continue to be, enshrouded with a similar sense of mystery and speculation.

Despite the earlier commitment to exploring a handful of Austen's single contemporaries, Lister, in fact, did not remain unmarried. In her classic Listerian fashion of making herself privy to the rights of men, she decided that she too should be permitted to marry a woman should she so desire, and did so with her partner, Ann Walker, in 1834. The couple conducted a private wedding ceremony at the Holy Trinity Church in York. Despite her *de facto* marriage status, Lister nonetheless succeeded in pursuing a life whereby her most intimate interactions with the opposite sex remained in the form of business transactions.

Lister's steadfast commitment to leading the life she so

desired was perhaps in part influenced by her visit to the home of the couple known as the Ladies of Llangollen. The owners of the house they named Plas Newydd, Lady Eleanor Butler (1739-1832) and Sarah Ponsonby (1755-1831), were members of the Irish aristocracy who, to avoid mounting pressures from their families to marry, ran away together. The pair sailed from Ireland to Wales In 1778, eventually setting up home together along with the maid who enabled their escape.

Much of their daily activity that followed is known thanks to Eleanor Butler's diary. Although it remains an important historical source that uniquely details the lives of two 18th-century women living without male partners in an all-female household, her diary remains on the mundane side, especially when compared to Lister's musings. Butler's diary swaps Lister's elicit romantic interests and covert sexual encounters for the banalities of domestic life and the idleness of long-term partnership. At times, Butler writes, the pair would stay 'in the library the entire day,' sheltering from the rain in each other's company. The frequent occasions where Butler refers to her partner as 'my beloved' and 'my Sarah' is the most telling evidence from her diaries that the two were involved romantically, and did not traverse the Irish sea to subsequently share a life together simply because they were very dear friends. Having said this, their decision to name not one, but a succession of their dogs, Sappho, is indeed rather telling. Upon visiting the two women, Lister wrote to a lover at the time that she thought it unlikely the couple had a purely 'platonic' relationship.

Fellow champion of female coupledom, Lister, was not the only inspired fan to travel the country with the desire to meet the couple and bear witness to their unusual set-up first-hand. Fascinated by the banal domesticities of two loving Irish ladies and their pet dogs, the pair's North Wales home inspired keen visitors from across the country, including the likes of William Wordsworth and the Duke of Wellington.

Discovering Pride in Austen's Time

The couple lived together for 50 years, committed to a shared life of reading, learning languages, and occasionally, inviting in keen onlookers for a view of an alternative life. They passed away within two years of each other.

Another notable mention is Anne Seymour Damer (1748-1828), whose life was defined not only by her choice of romantic company but by her professional aspirations, too. She was known for her career as a sculptor at a time when women in this field were few and far between. Her status as a member of high society, however, no doubt enabled this pursuit, allowing her to pursue lessons in art and anatomy – a subject that most women were barred from studying.

Admittedly, Damer's brief marriage which ended when she was 27 following her husband's death, should arguably have disqualified her from inclusion in an essay that professes an interest in exploring unmarried contemporaries of Austen. However, the single life she lived as a widow is worthy of recognition, and the notoriety she gained as a consequence almost eclipses her earlier married status.

It was not only her sculpting endeavours that cast her out from the other high-society women of her day. Satirists and notable voices speculated frequently about her involvement with other women, with local newspapers and periodicals referring to her as the 'Sapphic Sculptress.' She was even described by writer Hester Piozzi as 'a lady much suspected for liking her own sex in a criminal way' – a suspicion that unsurprisingly complicated and damaged her relations with women in her social sphere.

The most significant partner to whom Damer expressed her 'criminal' affections most ardently, and shared the last 30 years of her life with, was writer and intellectual, Mary Berry. Although rumours spread concerning the nature of their relationship, the couple were fortunate enough to inherit the gothic-style castle Strawberry Hill House in Twickenham, a residence designed by

Encounters with Jane Austen

Damer's godfather, Horace Walpole (1717-1797). Strawberry Hill House provided the couple an opportunity to live together and gain some privacy away from rumour, scandal, and ridicule.

Similarly to the other women mentioned, the nature of the couple's relationship can be understood now through the letters that Damer and Berry shared with one another. Thanks largely to their content, many of Damer's letters avoided the same fate as Austen's. Despite requesting that her letters expressing her 'criminal' love for her own sex be burned after her death, Berry, unable to part with her late partner's words, kept a handful of them. They remain to this day in the British Museum, fragments of a passion once ridiculed and satirised now preserved, and hopefully looked upon with dignity.

It is important to mention that, while the women in focus here flew in the face of societal convention and were often presented with criticism and mockery in return, their class status did much to enable their freedom to subvert the conventions of the day. There is no doubt that, running parallel to the individuals discussed here are a large number of less financially fortunate women, compelled into marriage but with a strong desire to be free of it – perhaps with a yearning to pass their days in the company and the loving arms of another woman.

To conclude, this short exploration of Jane Austen and her unmarried, female-loving, fringe of society contemporaries, has steered well clear of making any baseless assumptions of queerness lurking within, or expressed by, the late author.

These musings aim to place Austen within a context, to highlight women of her time who, too, pursued an untraditional, female-centred life, and in so doing, to assert that the late author was not alone. And thus, it just so happens that a small proportion of the population would, like Austen, turn down a Mr Darcy in favour of a life of beautiful prose and female companionship.

Discovering Pride in Austen's Time

Caitlin Grills is a writer and editor with an interest in Eastern European politics. She previously edited *Slovo* Journal for UCL, an international The journal publishes original research articles and reviews within the field of Slavic languages, literatures and cultures.

Caitlin completed an MA in Russian Studies at UCL, and an MSt in English 1813-1940 at University of Oxford.

Three of Diamonds[1]

Stephanie Lyttle

Logged
in remnants, a world
no cartographer charts. Years
in blood red, bud green, blush pink,
bitter ecru. Now, entombed in white tissue,
a bride awaits the touch of her curator.
Unseized by death, here lies
a shrine to my sister's
missed stitch.

Like
good sentences,
stitches, too, have their syntax.
How will this quilt be read when we are gone?
Will they divine the soft soul blue of our ducks' eggs,
the midday ochre of our sunflowers, storeys tall?
Will they understand just how long
those bright springs
spooled on?

---

[1] After the Austen women's patchwork coverlet https://janeaustens.house/object/patchwork-coverlet/

Three of Diamonds

Time
is a running stitch.
Time is a blank page, a blink,
waxing aster, waning strawberries,
the rhythm of growings, losings, leavings.
Time is a painting with the sketch showing through,
measured in throat-clearing and after-dinner talk.
I pack my hourglass with petals, but I know
time is a soft fruit rotting on the stalk.
One season a ruby,
the next

—

Stephanie Lyttle is a part-time PhD student in Creative Writing, specialising in writing fiction for young adults. She has won various awards and funding for her work, including Arts and Humanities Research Council PhD funding, the Grierson Prize for verse, and New Writing North's Creative Associates funding. She was previously a poet in residence for Jane Austen's House, which inspired 'Three of Diamonds'.

Mansfield Park[1]

Julia Quinn

I am an author of historical romances, which means that I spend an inordinate amount of time in front of my computer, dreaming of witty men, wittier women, and ways to torture them both before allowing a happily-ever-after. I know the difference between a duke and an earl (and the proper way to address each, both in person and in writing), and I regularly find myself researching such strange and random bits of knowledge as the journey length from Liverpool to Dublin in 1819, the location of Boucher's Portrait of Marie-Louise O'Murphy during the same year, and the earliest known usage of the phrase "Little Bo Peep." (At least twelve hours, Germany, and Shakespeare, as far as I can tell.)

Like most authors writing in my time period, I worship at the altar of Jane Austen, and while I do not credit her with the birth of the modern romance novel (what she did and what I do are far too dissimilar for that), she must be acknowledged as the genre's most vital and influential ancestor. I hadn't read *Mansfield Park*, although I was aware that it was considered Jane Austen's most difficult and least popular novel. I immediately contacted my brother, a poet and academic who has much more experience with literary analysis and response than I do. His excitement was palpable. *Mansfield Park* was not your usual Austen novel. It was complicated. It was hard. It was far more than mere entertainment. Here was my chance to get romance readers into Austen, and from there they might move on to someone even more esoteric, like James Joyce or William

[1] Originally published as an Afterword to *Mansfield Park* by Jane Austen in 2008 by Signet, an imprint of Penguin Publishing Group.

Mansfield Park

Faulkner. I declined to tell him that most of my readers were already into Austen, and that Joyce makes me want to open a vein. (Don't even get me started on Faulkner, whom I firmly believe could have used a lesson in punctuation.) My brother's excitement made me nervous; this is a man who reads Nietzsche for fun. But we were talking about Jane Austen. My inspiration. My muse.

My heroine.

Heroines are important to me, both in life and in fiction. This runs somewhat counter to current literary trends; most analysis of the modern romance novel focuses on the hero as the emotional centre of the book. And it is true that the author will get nowhere if she can't make the reader fall in love with the hero.

In her essay "The Androgynous Reader: Point of View in the Romance," found in the seminal collection *Dangerous Men and Adventurous Women: Romance Writers on the Appeal of Romance*, Laura Kinsale puts forth the heroine-as-placeholder theory. Her clearest argument, and one I largely agree with, comes at the expense of *Shanna*, a massive 1977 bestseller by Kathleen E. Woodiwiss:

"A sillier and more wrong-headed heroine would be difficult to imagine; very few women would go to bed dreaming of actually resembling the annoying little shrew. Ah, but to be in her place – that is another matter."

Unlike Austen, Woodiwiss can be credited with the birth of the modern romance novel. Her 1972 novel *The Flame and the Flower* was like nothing readers had ever experienced. Pulled from the slush pile at Avon Books, it went on to sell over two million copies in its first four years on sale. Her books opened the bedroom door within the narrative, and if her heroines were occasionally annoying, her heroes were larger than life, and indeed, every reader wanted the thrill of bringing him to his knees.

Encounters with Jane Austen

In other words, it was all about the hero.

Kinsale further explains her theory by contrasting placeholding and reader identification:

"Placeholding and reader identification should not be confused. Placeholding is an objective involvement; the reader rides along with the character, having the same experiences but accepting or rejecting the character's actions, words, and emotions on the basis of her personal yardstick. Reader identification is subjective: the reader becomes the character, feeling what she or he feels, experiencing the sensation of being under control of the character's awareness."

When I first started writing, I knew I wanted to put more focus on the heroine. Why was it, I wondered, that romance heroines so infrequently had female friends? The hero had his brother or best buddy (who was then spun off as a hero of a later book), but the heroine almost always began the narrative in emotional isolation. Readers complain that romance heroines too often fit one of two archetypes: the annoyingly defiant beauty or the doormat. But without any type of support system, how could she be anything else?

I wanted a romance in which the heroine was more than a placeholder. I wanted that sense of reader identification. This is where Austen succeeds so handily in most of her novels. Don't we all adore Elizabeth Bennet? She is sharp, she is witty. She is not perfect, but that just makes her more familiar. And when we are lost in *Pride and Prejudice*, we want to *be* her, not just be in her place. We want to deliver that witty rebuke at the proper time (and not thirty minutes later, which is when the rest of us usually think of something so clever). We want Jane as our sister and best friend, and oh yes, we want a man who tells us he loves us.

Most ardently.

I don't just love Elizabeth Bennet. I want to be Elizabeth Bennet. Everyone wants to be Elizabeth Bennet, or if not that,

Mansfield Park

then a Dashwood sister or a loveable meddler named Emma.

And therein lies *Mansfield Park's* problem, because no one wants to be Fanny Price.

It's not even that we don't want her situation, although it's true, we don't. She is the quintessential poor relation, given next to nothing and expected to be grateful for it. She is trapped between two worlds – the grandeur and position of *Mansfield Park,* where she is informed every day, and in a hundred different ways, that she will never quite belong; and her childhood home in Portsmouth, which lingers wistfully in her imagination until she returns as an adult and finds it coarse and untidy. Fanny has no place, no true anchor. An unenviable situation indeed.

But this could be forgiven by the reader. Literature is full of beloved underdogs. No, the problem with Fanny is that no one actually likes Fanny. She is timid, gets winded if she walks across a lawn, and when she works up the nerve to speak, she is often priggish and judgmental. She is not, in any sense, a romantic heroine.

And yet she's the one who gets the guy in the end.

Much has been made of the contrast between Fanny Price and Mary Crawford, Fanny's rival for Edmund's affections. Mary is everything Fanny is not: worldly, witty, athletic, and adaptable. Mary has all the good lines; Fanny's dialogue is often thoughtful and intelligent, but she can only rarely be called clever. Indeed, more than one reader has wondered why Austen did not simply make Mary her heroine. She exists on the page nearly as much as Fanny, and she is certainly far more engaging to the reader. She can be shallow, yes, but she also frequently exhibits acts of kindness toward Fanny that show her nature to be far more perceptive and unselfish than she is often given credit for.

One of Fanny's greatest moments of distress occurs when first Tom, and then Maria and Mr Crawford, pressure her to take a role in *Lovers' Vows*, the amateur theatrical being staged at Mansfield during Sir Thomas's absence. Fanny holds firm, and the onslaught is capped by a blistering attack from her aunt Norris:

"I am not going to urge her" – replied Mrs Norris sharply, "but I shall think her a very obstinate, ungrateful girl, if she does not do what her aunt and cousins wish her – very ungrateful indeed, considering who and what she is."

Here it is Mary, and not Edmund (who is rendered speechless), who comes to Fanny's aid: "... Miss Crawford looking for a moment with astonished eyes at Mrs Norris, and then at Fanny, whose tears were beginning to show themselves, immediately said with some keenness, "I do not like my situation; this place is too hot for me" – and moved away her chair to the opposite side of the table close to Fanny, saying to her in a kind low whisper as she placed herself, "Never mind, my dear Miss Price – this is a cross evening – everyone is cross and teasing – but do not let us mind them"; and with pointed attention continued to talk to her and endeavor to raise her spirits, in spite of being out-of-spirits herself…"

At the end, however, and in bits and pieces along the way, Mary reveals herself as lacking the moral core required for an Austen heroine. Most of her transgressions are minor, and indeed, only serve to make Fanny and Edmund less likable for their criticism of her. But her reaction to Henry and Maria's affair, as recounted by Edmund, crosses a fatal literary boundary, and she cannot be redeemed:

"She saw it only as folly, and that folly stamped only by exposure... it was the detection in short – Oh! Fanny, it was the detection, not the offence which she reprobated."

It is here that the critical distinction between Mary and Fanny is drawn. Austen – and Edmund – and indeed the reader might have forgiven Mary her lack of gravity had she acknowledged the true nature and depth of Henry and Maria's sins. It is difficult to imagine any of Austen's other heroines, despite their flaws, behaving in such a manner.

But I find myself uncomfortable calling Fanny the heroine of *Mansfield Park*, either. There are a number of indications that she is meant to be; she is the central character of the first several chapters of the book (even if she herself says and does very little). And certainly there would not be much of a story if Fanny had not been brought to Mansfield by her wealthier relations. She is a linchpin; without Fanny, Henry Crawford would have no moral awakening. (Some might argue that her rejection of his suit leads to his moral relapse, as well.) Without Fanny as a foil to Maria and Julia, Sir Thomas would not fully realize the extent of his daughters' shallowness, and by extension his own culpability as their parent.

But a heroine? I think not. Set against today's romantic standards, she certainly does not measure up. Romance heroines have evolved; Fanny needn't fit into a preset stereotype to succeed in this literary endeavour, but she needs something – anything – to endear her to the reader. We want to root for someone. Yes, we follow Fanny's silent and unrequited love for Edmund, but our interest flags; Edmund is dull, and Fanny is duller. We want the good guys to win, but there is little satisfaction to be had if the good guys are boring.

The simple explanation for this would be that despite the nuptials at the end of the story, *Mansfield Park* is not a romance, and thus it would be foolish to expect Fanny to fulfill the role of the romantic heroine. This is certainly true; it is difficult to imagine that even Austen saw her novel as a romance. There is no fabulous declaration of love between Edmund and Fanny; instead the narrator informs: "I only entreat everybody to believe that exactly at the time when it was quite natural that it should be so, and not a week earlier, Edmund did cease to care about Miss Crawford, and became as anxious to marry Fanny, as Fanny herself could desire."

Encounters with Jane Austen

This is not the stuff of romantic legend.

But even if we do not view *Mansfield Park* through the lens of romance, Fanny still serves as a very poor heroine. We can acknowledge that she is intelligent, and her ability to remain true to her own moral code must be admired, but Lionel Trilling was certainly on to something when he wrote, quite famously: "No one, I believe, has ever found it possible to like the heroine of *Mansfield Park*." It is telling that the only rendition of *Mansfield Park* in which Fanny emerges as a vibrant and well-loved character is the 1999 film adaptation by Patricia Rozema. In this version, Fanny is an aspiring writer, sending her breathless tales by post to her younger sister, Susan. Fanny of the page would have been appalled; this is the girl whose reaction to an amateur theatrical is agitation, condemnation, and redness of face. She does eventually come to find some entertainment in assisting with the production, but Austen makes it clear that Fanny could never bring herself to take part in so scandalous a creative endeavour.

Here, of course, lies the irony. The romantic stories ascribed to Fanny in Rozema's film are gleaned from the youthful writings of Jane Austen herself. Fanny has been transformed into a far more acceptable heroine by making her more like her creator. And yet it was that creator who, some two decades later, placed Fanny in *Mansfield Park* – a humourless protagonist in an uncharacteristically humourless book.

What, then, is the value of *Mansfield Park*? What does it mean to be the unpopular Jane Austen novel? I struggled with this question for some time; I did not enjoy *Mansfield Park* as much as I did Austen's other novels, and yet I cannot regret having read it. Or, more tellingly, having spent countless hours pondering its characters. I don't like Fanny, I find Edmund a bore, and I frequently disapprove of Mary. But I know them. And I know enough of Austen to think that this must have been her intention.

Mansfield Park

Modern writers communicate with readers in ways unfathomable to Austen and her contemporaries. The internet has turned the computer screen into one giant book club. We know what our readers want because they tell us, whether we wish to hear it or not. As an author, I walk a literary tightrope, searching for an acceptable balance between delivering the sort of story my readers anticipate and not writing the same book over and over again. Austen was not afforded the same sort of feedback that authors of today enjoy (or not), but she had to have realized that in *Mansfield Park* she had created a novel fundamentally different from those that preceded it. She was far too astute to think that her readers would take to Fanny as they had to Lizzie Bennet. And who (besides Fanny) could ever love Edmund with Mr. Darcy waiting in the wings?

I can only conclude that *Mansfield Park* suffers under the weight of reader expectation – a challenge more commonly faced by authors of genre fiction. A romance must end happily. A mystery must be solved. And a Jane Austen novel must sparkle. Which is why *Mansfield Park* so frequently disappoints. It does not sparkle; it rarely even entertains. B ut in its quiet, subversive way, it lingers.

Julia Quinn is a best-selling American author whose novels have been translated into 43 languages. She has been inducted into the Romance Writers of America Hall of Fame. Her *Bridgerton* book series has been adapted for Netflix into a television series of the same name produced by Shondaland. Quinn won the Romance Writers of America RITA Award, in 2007, for *On the Way to the Wedding* and again, in 2008 for *The Secret Diaries of Miss Miranda Cheever* and 2010 for *What Happens in London*.

"We have all a better guide
in ourselves, if we would
attend to it, than any
other person
can be."

– Mansfield Park

A Zuihitsu on Various Walks

Ellora Sutton

I walk, my mother walked. It's how the women in my family exert their soft power – in turns and strides.

*

Yesterday I walked nine miles through London for a friend's book launch, and noticed almost nothing –

a girl blowing bubbles into the sky
over her flat's walkway, brown brick
protecting her from the sky, the street beneath.
A sign in a jeweller's window saying FEED THE BIRDS,
another: by appointment only.
Bloomsbury Square. Cheapside. Brick Lane.
Churros, the smell and sound of them –
Prêt A Manger, Prêt A Manger, Prêt A Manger.
Wisteria spilling like champagne and music
from windows; Sophie Ellis-Bextor, twice.
A sign on a tree telling us to enjoy the trees,
they won't be here forever.

*

A flâneuse is a woman who walks for the sake of walking,

not to go anywhere in particular but to be somewhere. To wander, and wonder.

The male equivalent of the flâneuse is the flâneur. Some people say it's impossible for there to be a female version of the flâneur because it requires anonymity, and a woman is incapable of passing unseen in the urban environment.

*

How often have I, as a young woman, been told not to go walking (alone) in a certain place, or at a certain time, or looking like that –

> *she really looked*
> *almost wild*

*

I watch an elderly man in a blue-and-white striped shirt, reading on a park bench. His paperback is yellowed and floppy. A crow struts through the daisies and buttercups; the grass barely signifies. When the crow gets closer to him, the man reads out loud.

I'm too far away to hear individual words, receive only their mouth-feel.

Despite my hefty copy of *BURN IT DOWN! Feminist Manifestos for the Revolution*, the man comes over. As so often happens, he has mistaken my noticing for a desire to be noticed. He has mistaken me for a student, which also happens often – I think it's the way I look around at things, and my glasses, the omnipresence of books and notebooks, even here, at this picnic table.

A Zuihitsu on Various Walks

He asks what I'm studying, if he can buy me a coffee from the nearby kiosk.

she had carefully avoided every companion on her rambles

He has a kind face.

I decline the coffee, but talk to him a while anyway. I tell him that I'm writing about walking, and Jane Austen, and also about Jane Austen and walking. I don't tell him that, up until a few minutes ago, that meant writing about him.

Yesterday he went walking in Winchester, and saw Jane Austen's grave.

*

When I am walking, or wandering, I am edgeless. I am winged. I could be anywhere, anywhen.

*

a beautiful walk
home by Moonlight

My favourite memory is a field.
There was a snail in the tall grass,
and no clouds.

her fine eyes were brightened
by the exercise

*

Encounters with Jane Austen

Walking by the pond, I stop to smell the wild garlic
bruised by the sun's need to hold everything close.
The air sparkles with the ceaseless clink gnats.
The wild garlic falls on either side of the path,
like after a wedding,
and the light through the trees make me feel ancient –
that goose blocking my way might really be a god,
a goddess, a personification of something lost
or something returning.

*

I walk from the public gardens to the bookshop where my name hangs in a blue plaque above the bar. I pass through so many smells, and I smell all of them, I am a hound. The pizza places – Domino's, Papa Johns, Caprinos – are just waking up. Windows are being cleaned.

I drink the coolest, crispest glass of Diet Coke ever. They give it to me in a wine glass full of ice. Women of all ages are eating cake and reading. We can be unseen here, and together.

Truthfully, I don't know which I prefer – the smell of wild garlic, or the smell of garlic bread.

*

My feet ache in their boots. I can feel the red of city-walking in my thighs, the chafe and refusal to give.

such desperate walkers

It's in my body.

A Zuihitsu on Various Walks

*

As we cross Paper Mill Lane to the train station, I notice a snail in the road, peeling and unpeeling itself along the tarmac.

It's early, but already hot. There are cars, yes, rush-hour dregs, but not close, not yet.

I have time.

Gently as picking a blackberry, I pick the snail up by its shell and ferry it over to a community planter on the other side.

My companion calls me reckless, says my life is worth more than a snail.

I have never been so in my body.

Notes: This is based on recent walks in and around places Jane Austen herself walked, both urban and rural – London, Alton, and Chawton. "she really looked almost wild" and "her fine eyes were brightened by the exercise" are taken from *Pride and Prejudice*. "she had carefully avoided every companion on her rambles" is taken from *Sense and Sensibility*. "a beautiful walk home by Moonlight" is quoted from a letter Jane Austen wrote to her sister Cassandra, dated 8th September 1816. "ceaseless clink" is from *Persuasion*, describing the city sounds of Bath: "the dash of other carriages, the heavy rumble of carts and drays, the bawling of newspapermen, muffin-men and milkmen, and the ceaseless clink of pattens" – pattens were a kind of raised overshoe that women could wear when walking in inclement weather. "such desperate walkers" is quoted from a letter from Jane to Cassandra, dated 30th November 1800 – the "desperate walkers" in question are Jane and her friend Martha Lloyd.

Encounters with Jane Austen

'A Zuihitsu on Various Walks', was written for National Walking Month in May 2024, and was one of the last pieces of work I did as the Creative Engagement Officer at Jane Austen's House – the House, as I often told visitors, where Jane Austen spent the last eight years of her life; living here she wrote or re-wrote all six of her main novels, and it's living here that she became a published author for the very first time. That's the introduction I used to give to visitors, back when I first started at Jane Austen's House, not as the Creative Engagement Officer but as a Visitor Services Assistant. It was my first job out of university, aged 21, selling replica gold-and-turquoise rings in the gift shop and selling tickets to walk-up visitors. When I got the job, I cried. I'd always wanted to work at a museum, but to get to work in the home of my absolute hero? If you're the sort of person who reads an anthology of writing about Jane Austen, then I'm sure I don't need to tell you that it was a dream come true.

I worked at Jane Austen's House (in the picture-perfect village of Chawton, Hampshire) for six years, which is a long amount of time in your twenties. It feels a bit like I grew up there. During that time I did a part-time master's, published two poetry pamphlets, fell in love, had my heart broken, and met thousands of fellow Austenites.

Living in Hampshire, about ten minutes away from the House, it was hard to escape the pull of Austen – even if I never did study her at school. My first encounter with Jane Austen and her House was age fifteen, a matter of months after my mother had died, a trip with my auntie and grandmother in bright summer sunshine. I'd never read Austen before, I didn't even know the plot of *Pride and Prejudice*. It's a testament to the excellent work at the House, especially the enthusiasm and warmth of the volunteer stewards, that I left utterly enchanted, with a new hero. I threw myself into reading her novels, starting with a £1.99 paperback copy of *Pride and Prejudice* with Hugh Thompson's iconic illustrations; my grandmother

A Zuihitsu on Various Walks

bought it for me in the House giftshop. Austen's sharp wit and vivid characters gave me a world to escape into at the exact moment when I needed an escape the most. I remember reading *Mansfield Park* and feeling so utterly seen. I identified deeply with Fanny Price, the lonely, unsettled teenage girl who pays deep attention to the world around her – although now I'd like to imagine myself as more of a Mary Crawford. These characters felt like friends, and so did their writer. I think it helped, in my state of grief, that out of Austen's heroines, those that don't have a dead mother at least suffer from an absent or inadequate one. Amongst Austen, I wasn't othered by my loss.

It's funny, isn't it, how Austen devotees genuinely feel that they have a very real, almost parasocial, relationship with Jane Austen. I witnessed it every day at work. People who step foot into the giftshop/ticket office and start to cry. People who feel passionately about and advocate for the version of Austen they've constructed in their head – for example, those who reject Cassandra Austen's portrait as 'too ugly' to be their Jane, as if they understand better the appearance of Austen based on six novels and scant letters than her own sister did. But I digress. This is not a criticism – far from it – in fact, I think it's a testament to Austen's genius that there are as many 'Jane Austens' out there as there are readers of her work. She meets each reader where they are, even 250 years later. In my experience, each encounter with a reader brings a new encounter with Jane Austen.

I got to do so much and meet so many people (and their Janes) as Creative Engagement Officer at Jane Austen's House. Leading school trips around the House, fielding mischievous/disruptive questions from teenagers who'd rather be somewhere else reminded me of Jane Austen's own wit and standoffishness in the face of authority. Facilitating virtual book clubs over Zoom, where people would join from all over the world for an hour to discuss their favourite novels, where distance just evaporated away and we were all sat there, in a cozy drawing room, ready to defend our problematic favourite characters and air our own hot takes. Dressing up in costumes – my favourite was a yellow and gold ballgown that I had to be safety-pinned into – always added a touch of magic to proceedings. Watching the village cats sunning themselves in the courtyard on my lunchbreak. I got to explore Austen through all different lenses, such as being able to explore elements of my own identity writing pieces for Pride Month. My proudest moment, though, was getting to curate my own mini exhibition, 'Obstinate, Headstrong Girls', a celebration of the real-life women whom Austen knew and was, perhaps, inspired by, including her cousin Eliza de Feuillide (who married a French count and narrowly avoided the French Revolution), her mentor Madam Lefroy (who, among many other things, single-handedly vaccinated over 800 of her husband's parishioners against smallpox), and her mother Mrs Cassandra Austen (who managed a 200-acre farm alongside raising eight children). A digital version of the exhibition is still available online, and if that's my legacy I'll be more than happy.

After six years, I left Jane Austen's House to pursue a PhD in English – I'm using poetry as a practice-based research method to assess how women experience heritage sites (such as museums and galleries) as walkable spaces, which in many ways feels like a natural continuation of aspects of my previous work. Austen still pops up in my conversations at least daily; I often joke that she 'haunts' me. I can't think about cheese, for example, without also thinking about Austen writing a Christmastime letter about receiving an anonymous half a Stilton cheese, presumably from her (favourite) brother Henry, and/or the story about a prospective suitor trying to impress Austen by ordering a plate of toasted cheese (her favourite food) up to her room.

I went to my first conference as a PhD student a couple of weeks back. I felt way out of my depth, almost too nervous

A Zuihitsu on Various Walks

to talk to anyone – that is, until I spotted a young woman carrying a tote bag with a Hugh Thompson illustration from *Persuasion* on it. Hey, I said, I like your bag. I'm an Austen fan too. Is *Persuasion* your favourite?

If you know Jane Austen, you will always have a friend, anywhere you go.

Photo: Thom Bartley for *Verve*

Ellora Sutton is a PhD candidate using poetry as a practice-based research method to explore how women experience museums as walkable urban spaces; prior to that, she was the Creative Engagement Officer at Jane Austen's House. She is the poetry reviewer for *Mslexia,* and her poems have appeared in *The Poetry Review, Oxford Poetry,* and *Berlin Lit* etc. Her pamphlets include *Antonyms for Burial* (Poetry Book Society Spring 2023 Pamphlet Choice) and, most recently, *Artisanal Slush*. She has been poet-in-residence at Jane Austen's House and Petersfield Museum.

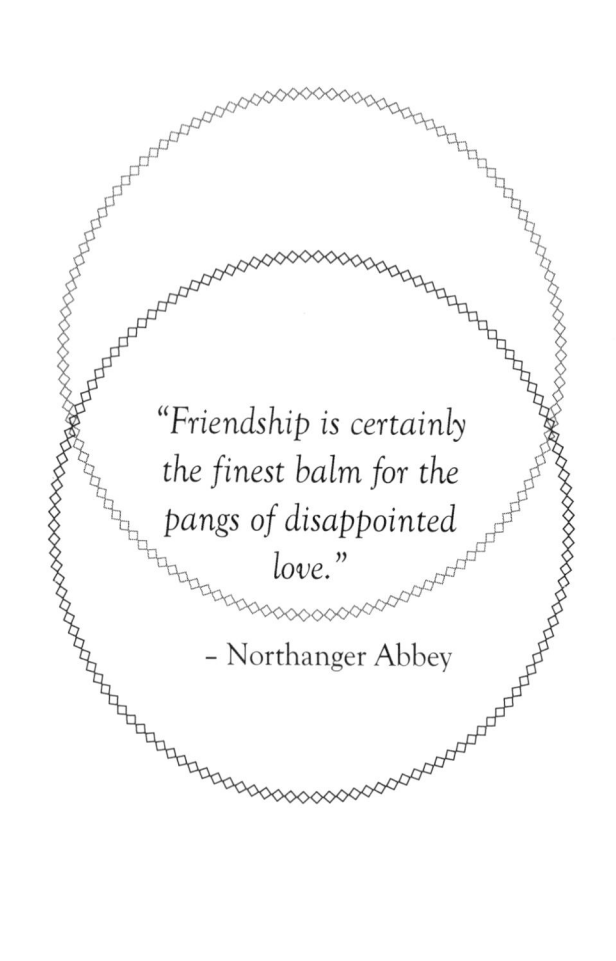

"Friendship is certainly the finest balm for the pangs of disappointed love."

– Northanger Abbey

They entered the breakfast room

First Impressions

[Chapter One]

Charlie Lovett

Steventon, Hampshire, 1796

Fond as she was of solitary walks, Jane had been wandering rather longer than she had intended, her mind occupied not so much with the story she had lately been reading as with one she hoped soon to be writing. She was shaken from this reverie by the sight of an unfamiliar figure, sitting on a stile, hunched over a book. Her first impression was that he was the picture of gloom – dressed in shabby clerical garb, a dark look on his crinkled face, doubtless a volume of dusty sermons clutched in his ancient hand. Even the weather seemed to agree with this assessment, for while the sun shone all around him, he sat in the shadow of the single cloud that hung in the Hampshire sky. Realizing how far she had come from home, Jane thought it best to retrace her steps without interrupting the cleric's thoughts as he had unknowingly interrupted hers. During the long walk home across the fields, shimmering with the haze of summer heat, she amused herself by sketching out a character of this old man, storing him away, like so many others, for possible inclusion in some novel yet to be conceived. He was, she decided, a natural history enthusiast, but his passion lay not with anything beautiful like butterflies or wildflowers. No, his particular expertise was in the way of garden slugs, of which he could identify twenty-six varieties.

By week's end, Jane had filled in the pathetic details of his

First Impressions

life. Disappointed in love, he had turned to natural history, where the objects of his pursuit were less likely to spurn his advances. As his passion for his study grew, and as he shared it more enthusiastically with those around him, his invitations to dine gradually declined until he was left alone on most evenings with his books and his slugs. He was a melancholy figure, which made it all the more shocking to find him, on Sunday morning, not only seated in the Austen family pew, but smiling broadly and greeting her by name.

Jane had led the family procession from the rectory to the small stone church of St. Nicholas, where her father was rector. The church stood on the far outskirts of the village, flanked by flat, green meadows. After passing through the rectory gates into the narrow lane that led to the church, the Austens had fallen in with several villagers. When she had concluded her pleasantries with these acquaintances, Jane had not a moment to respond to the stranger's greeting before the service began and she found herself separated from him by her mother and her sister, Cassandra; of her six brothers, none were currently in residence in Steventon.

The man's robust baritone voice, evident in his hymn singing, exuded a spirit that was anything but melancholy. Jane endured a sharp elbow from Cassandra for not attending to the gospel reading; instead, she was trying to watch the man out of the corner of her eye. She failed to follow the thread of her father's sermon, lost as she was in a re-evaluation of the stranger's history. By the time the service ended she was thoroughly intrigued and determined to secure a proper introduction to satisfy her curiosity about the true nature of his character.

"Go along home and I shall wait for Father," she told her mother and Cassandra as they stood beside the ancient yew tree that clung to the west end of the church. Jane felt certain that a visiting clergyman with leave to occupy the Austen pew must be known to her father, and she expected Mr Austen to make the necessary introduction, so it came as a surprise when she felt a tap on her shoulder and turned to face the stranger, who addressed her in a cheerful voice.

"Miss Jane Austen, if I am not mistaken."

"You are at an advantage, sir," said Jane. "You know my name, but I do not know yours."

"Mansfield. Reverend Richard Mansfield at your service," he said with a slight bow. "But we have nearly met already."

"What can you mean, sir?"

"Only that two days ago you emerged from the waving grain of Lord Wintringham's field and stopped in your tracks when you spotted me reading on a stile just outside Busbury Park. At the time I conceived the idea that you were a rather dull and impetuous young lady, but I already begin to suspect that I may have been mistaken." His eyes twinkled in the morning sun as he said this, and his smile transformed from one meant for the general public to one that seemed to be reserved solely for Jane.

"I hope you will come to believe so, Mr Mansfield. I have been accused of having many faults by those who know me well, but neither dullness nor impetuousness has been among them."

"And what faults do they accuse you of?"

"My worst, or so I am told, are a too highly developed interest in fictionalizing my acquaintances and a tendency to form opinions of others hastily."

"Opinions such as the one you formed of me when you saw me alone with my book?"

"You do me wrong, sir. You assume first that I saw you, second that I gave your appearance sufficient thought to form an opinion, and third that my opinion was ill considered."

"In the first case," said Mr Mansfield, "I observed you

First Impressions

myself, for though your mind may have been elsewhere, your eyes were certainly on me; in the second case, your father tells me, somewhat to my surprise, that you aspire to write novels, so I can only assume that anyone you meet may become a victim of your imagination; and in the third case it seems impossible that you would have guessed the extent to which our interests overlap."

"I confess that shared interests did not occur to me. I imagined you a student of natural history, reading... but you will laugh when I tell you."

"I enjoy a good laugh," said Mr Mansfield.

"I imagined you reading a book on garden slugs."

Mr Mansfield did laugh, long and heartily, before confessing the true nature of his reading. "It may shock you, Miss Austen, but in fact I was reading a novel."

"A novel! You *do* shock me, sir. Do you not find novels full of nonsense? I myself find them the stupidest things in creation."

"Then you read novels?"

"Novels! I'm surprised at you, Mr Mansfield, suggesting that a young lady such as myself, the daughter of a clergyman, no less, could occupy her time with such horrid things as novels."

"You tease me, Miss Austen."

"Indeed I do not, Mr Mansfield, for though you know that I aspire to *write* novels, you cannot expect that I would take my interest in the form so far as to actually *read* them." Because Mr Mansfield was old enough to be her grandfather, Jane took the bold step of adding a wink to this statement and turned toward the rectory. The congregation had dispersed and only the sounds of birdsong and the breeze in the yew tree disturbed the silence of the morning. Jane was pleased when Mr Mansfield fell into step beside her as she made her way up

Encounters with Jane Austen

the tree-lined lane. With the summer sun now high in the sky, she was grateful for the cooling shade.

"Surely, Mr Mansfield, your shortest route to Busbury Park lies in the opposite direction," said Jane.

"Indeed it does, but you are assuming again, Miss Austen. First that I am staying at the park, and second that I am taking my luncheon there."

"And my novelist's imagination has deceived me again?"

"Not entirely," said Mr Mansfield. "For I am a guest at Busbury Park, but though he can offer me only cold mutton, your father has asked me to take my luncheon at the rectory."

"I confess, Mr Mansfield, I am sorry to hear it."

"And why is that? Are you so embarrassed to be seen in the company of a novel reader?"

"On the contrary, it is *because* you are a novel reader that I had rather hoped to keep you to myself. Once you enter the doors of the rectory, you will become a friend to my mother and my sister Cassandra, and you will no doubt retire after lunch to the study with my father and abandon the rest of us."

"Surely, Miss Austen," said Mr Mansfield, "I can be both a visitor at the rectory and a special friend of the rector's younger daughter."

"I believe, Mr Mansfield," said Jane as she took the clergyman's arm, "that I should like that very much indeed."

First Impressions

Charlie Lovett is the *New York Times* bestselling author of five novels including *The Bookman's Tale, First Impressions,* and *The Lost Book of the Grail.*

His plays for children have been seen in over 5,000 productions worldwide. His non-fiction works on Lewis Carroll include *Lewis Carroll: Formed by Faith* and the recently published definitive bibliography of Carroll's works. For five years he hosted the podcast *Inside the Writer's Studio*, interviewing authors from international bestsellers to debut novelists. He lives in Winston-Salem, NC, USA and spends several weeks a year in Kingham, Oxfordshire.

Tom Lefroy devours a Cotillion[1]

Marcelle Newbold

Handsome in her ankle skim gown,
thick pink ribbon snug under breasts,
a peek of lace at the spill of exposure
    her dress falls in exquisite folds–
the white of mistletoe, of snow wings.

Her fingers flex, held now within the veil
of her long leather gloves, she slowly opens
her fan across her negas bright face, opening
to conceal a slow taste of her still spiced lips.

A steady rhythm dissipates the heat,
it spreads with her every deliberate stroke.
Tom doesn't miss a step, attentive & eager,
    captivated he returns. Jane.

---

[1] A cotillion is a lively dance characterized by many intricate figures and the continual changing of partners.

Tom Lefroy devours a Cotillion

Marcelle Newbold's writing explores place and inheritance. Bridport Prize shortlisted, her poems have been published by *Poetry Wales, Propel, Ink Sweat & Tears, Black Bough Poetry, Indigo Dreams* and others.

Marcelle lives in Cardiff, Wales, and is a lifelong Jane Austen fan.

@marcellenewbold

www.marcellenewbold.co.uk

"Such very superior dancing is not often seen."

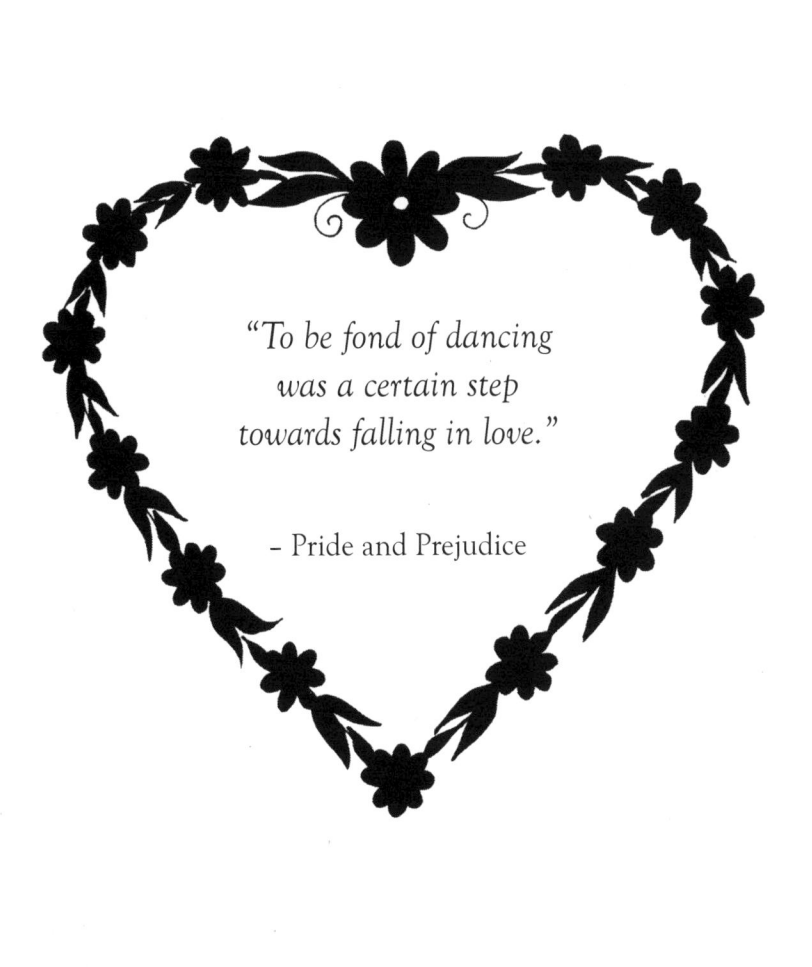

"To be fond of dancing was a certain step towards falling in love."

– Pride and Prejudice

Kipling's Tribute to Austen

Mary Hamer

The invitation to write about Jane Austen and what her work meant to me brought me up short. Though I knew her novels well, I realised I couldn't pass myself off as a real devotee. For one thing, it bothered me that her work had been taken up by some people for what seemed to me to be the wrong reasons, in the days before film versions widened her appeal by adding glamour. I'm talking about the well-heeled women – and men – I would sometimes hear enthusing over Jane Austen as 'so amusing'. They seemed to have adopted the novels as a sort of class accessory, like a handbag from Jermyn St.

I did appreciate her work but it's fair to say that my reading of it was formed in the context of formal education. *Emma* was one of my A Level texts and I've taught Austen to undergraduates. Yet today I never take a volume of hers down from the shelves, although her novels do continue to form part of my mental furniture: I was interested when attention started to be paid to the silent presence of the slave trade in *Mansfield Park* and to the Napoleonic Wars that form the background of her characters' lives but go unnamed. I was interested but it didn't draw me back to the novels. They never became old friends.

Worse, I recall that when I tried to read *Emma* again a few years ago I'd felt oddly numb, almost sedated. Also suspicious. The trouble is, I read differently nowadays: along with the rest of the world I've learned new languages in which to name what is going on within families. Old Mr Woodhouse, once presented to me as so charming, so harmless in his foibles, now looked to my eyes like a disaster for any daughter. If Emma

Kipling's Tribute to Austen

was unable to pick up the sexual vibes in the people around her, it was because her father was so physically absent, neutered. When Austen mocks Emma's complacency, Emma's confidence in her own reading of the world, it doesn't square with what I'm seeing. Austen's keen vision has allowed her to imagine the pairing of such a father with such a daughter and the negative impact on the developing girl. However, living when she did, Austen can command no terms in which to frame the damage to Emma beyond the language of 'good sense'.

I had a happier experience more recently when I picked up *Pride and Prejudice*. I saw exactly why Rudyard Kipling had praised her insight so highly, while Elizabeth's panache in fending off Lady Catherine delighted me. I began to wonder if I'd been missing years of happy Austen reading. But returning to *Persuasion*, generally described as the cream of the crop, disabused me. Nobody likes the way Sir Walter Elliot is presented as the novel opens: readers are told what to think of him instead of being allowed to find out for themselves. But as I read on, I found myself more and more uneasy about the way admiration for the heroine, Anne Elliot, is invited. Austen makes her stand out in comparison with the imperfect individuals who are her companions. I couldn't be doing with Anne's moral superiority and 'good sense': she is out to gently correct and improve everyone around her. Indifferent to her fate, I replaced the volume on the shelf.

No sooner had I done so, however, than it came back to me that Kipling, whom I did respond to, wrote both a short story and a poem in celebration of Austen.

Kipling noticed, as I had, how the gentry used reference to Austen as a code, a sign to indicate they were the right sort of people. In one sense he bases his story on that. Yet at heart, he is more deeply concerned with the human comfort brought by reading the novels in beloved company. He comes to identify this vital comfort amid the general suffering experienced during the Great War and its aftermath, years that bought him terrible personal loss. Nevertheless, for Kipling, comfort could be found in shared appreciation of the accuracy of Austen's vision. The poem he wrote about her celebrates that exceptional truthfulness.

So, to offer a more generous response to Austen and her works than my own, let me introduce the art she prompted from Rudyard Kipling.

> Jane went to Paradise:
>   That was only fair.
> Good Sir Walter followed her,
>   And armed her up the stair.
> Henry and Tobias,
>   And Miguel of Spain,
> Stood with Shakespeare at the top
>   To welcome Jane –

So begins the apparently whimsical poem, 'Jane's Marriage', which stands as introduction to Rudyard Kipling's story, 'The Janeites'. It goes on, through five stanzas and a coda, to imagine 'Jane' granted her heart's desire in Heaven – reunion with the original of Captain Wentworth. Only in the bold imagining of Seraphim on a hunt across the zodiac to find him can the range of a more familiar Kipling be found.

It might surprise some readers to find Austen's name linked with that of Kipling. The poem was composed to stand at the head of the story: he liked to preface his stories with a poem, a formal invention that was all his own. It's not always easy to grasp the connection between a particular poem and the story it heads. The challenge was deliberate, obliging readers to approach his theme from two different perspectives: in this

Kipling's Tribute to Austen

case, perhaps admiration for her perceptions and the comfort that reading her work could bring.

In 'The Janeites', written between 1922 and 1924, when it was published, Kipling takes his readers back to the experiences of the Great War of 1914-18 and to its aftermath: experiences and a scope that could seem to dwarf Austen's own narrow canvas. Nevertheless, the pivot of his story is the power of Austen's imagination. It tells how strangers were brought together across the lines of class and military rank by a shared passion for her novels. 'The Janeites' is a tale of connection and loyalty forged, not in battle, but behind the scenes of war.

The tale is set in a Freemason's Lodge on a Saturday afternoon in 1920: that is, a year or so after the close of the First World War. Members are joined in the weekly cleanup, a sort of housekeeping: giving a polish to the Masonic regalia, bringing a shine to the woodwork and floors. Within this framework, several stories of the war are layered. The link with Jane Austen is made through Humberstall, the survivor of two direct hits which have left his body intact but his mind prone to switching off into 'sort of quiet fits' – as Antony, a kindly fellow-Mason puts it. Encouraged by Antony to say more about a mysterious 'Jane', Humberstall tells how he came to observe that a dropped reference to Austen or her works could create a fellowship between other soldiers, one that cut across differences of rank.

Given the chance, he paid a gentleman private to coach him and read the novels in order to join in. Later, having suffered his second direct hit, attracting attention by comparing a nurse to Miss Bates got him on a hospital train, saving his life.

It's a work that has had its critics – some find the celebration of 'the Janeites' smug and fundamentally conservative: contradictory, in fact, as upholding the differences of class and rank it purports to present as melting away. I have some sympathy for that view. Yet, for me, it is important that by

Encounters with Jane Austen

the end of the tale, Austen's novels are providing Humberstall with comfort and a means to survive, psychologically, in the peace. For Humberstall is a mourner: the second direct hit he was in wiped out a small society that had been his world, the little group of men thrown together in and around the officers' mess. There remains one consolation: he's still got Jane Austen. "I read all her six books now for pleasure …an' it brings it all back – down to the smell of the glue-paint on the (camouflage) screens."

The Kipling who sat down to write Humberstall's story was also a mourner. What makes this story appeal to me is the sense of how much was at stake for him in writing it. Look at a timeline and you can trace how his particular experience of reading Austen was interleaved with his own struggle to recover after devastating loss.

March 1915: he's reading Jane Austen and announces that for the first time he is sure she's greater than Scott or Dickens in the way she peoples her novels. He pinpoints the fact that her characters are not invented. Instead, they are drawn from the experience of everyday as observed with an exceptional insight that meant motivation lay open to her. As a writer, language was her tool: Kipling saw her at work like a surgeon, with "a more delicate hand and a keener scalpel" than the other novelists.

August 1915: his only son, John, is killed in action at WWI's Battle of Loos.

Kipling has been blamed for that: not so. Let me set the record straight. When his poor sight got John rejected, he was so desperate to go to war that he had threatened to sign up as a private soldier. Knowing that men in the ranks were lasting only a matter of weeks before being killed or wounded, his father pulled strings to get him a commission as an officer. The longer training officers received would at least delay his being sent out to France.

Kipling's Tribute to Austen

January 1917: his wife Carrie writes in her diary that in the evenings her husband was reading Jane Austen's novels aloud to their daughter, Elsie, and herself "to our great delight".

1922–23 he is writing 'The Janeites'.

*

I see him in 1917, as returning in spirit to March 1915, that time of pleasure and confidence, and to the writer whose keen insight into everyday women and men delighted him with its truth. At that time John was still alive and their family intact. Now, in 1917, John dead, by going back to Austen his father recreates the pleasure her accurate perceptions had given him. He also shares that, by reading her work aloud to comfort his depleted family.

When he sits down to write 'The Janeites' in 1922 with the war well past, it is from the well of these experiences, transformed, that Kipling draws the story of Humberstall, with its homely setting in the cleanup, its nostalgia for the lost intimacy of the mess. The writer underlines how for that fictional survivor too, the wonder of Austen's novels lies in their truthful representation of human behaviour. Humberstall can match her characters against his direct experience:

"They was only just like people you run across any day. One of 'em was a curate – the Reverend Collins – always on the make an' lookin' to marry money. Well, when I was a Boy Scout, 'im or 'is twin brother was our troop-leader."

Encounters with Jane Austen

Mary Hamer taught at Cambridge before taking up fellowships at Harvard. She is a cultural historian, publishing widely on representation as it intersects with politics and history. Topics include the image of Cleopatra and the understanding of incest and abuse. Her novel *Kipling & Trix*, about Kipling and his sister, was awarded the Virginia Prize for Fiction.

Whenever she spoke in a low voice

Buried Love

Sara Teasdale

I have come to bury Love
Beneath a tree,
In the forest tall and black
Where none can see.

I shall put no flowers at his head,
Nor stone at his feet,
For the mouth I loved so much
Was bittersweet.

I shall go no more to his grave,
For the woods are cold.
I shall gather as much of joy
As my hands can hold.

I shall stay all day in the sun
Where the wide winds blow,
But oh, I shall cry at night
When none will know.

Buried Love

Sara Teasdale (1884-1933) was an American lyric poet. She was born in St. Louis, Missouri. From 1904 to 1907, Teasdale was a member of The Potters, led by Lillie Rose Ernst, a group of young female artists who published, *The Potter's Wheel,* a monthly literary magazine in St. Louis. Teasdale was courted by the performance poet Vachel Lindsay, who had no regular income and, due to his inability to offer her financial stability, they never married. In 1914, Sara chose to marry a wealthy businessman by the name of Ernst Filsinger and they moved to New York in 1916.

Teasdale's third poetry collection, *Rivers to the Sea,* was published in 1915 and became a bestseller. In 1918, she won a Pulitzer Prize for her 1917 poetry collection *Love Songs.* Her marriage to Filsinger broke down and they divorced in 1929. In 1931, Lindsay fell into a depression and died by suicide. Teasdale took a fatal overdose of sleeping pills in 1933.

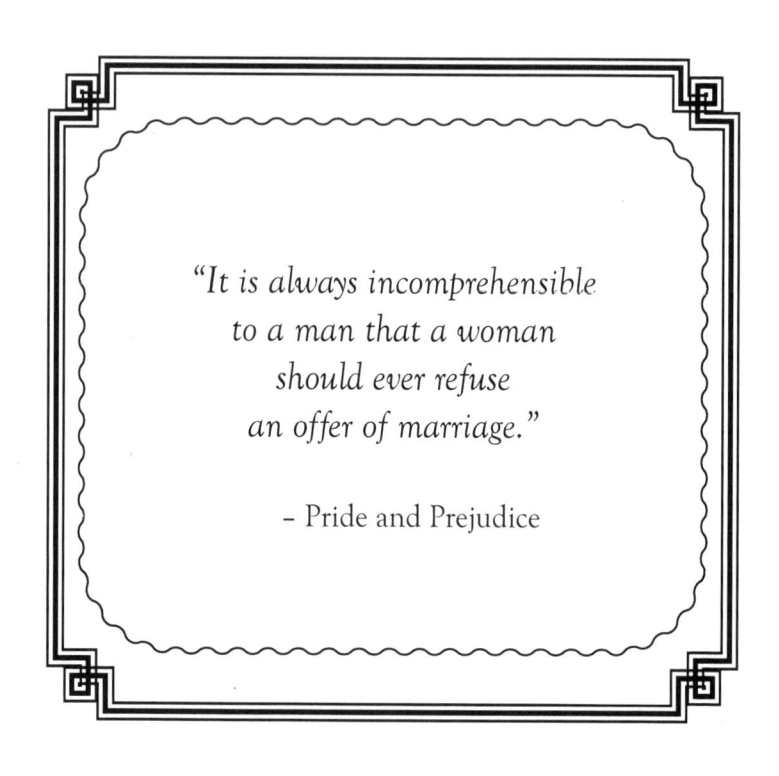

"It is always incomprehensible to a man that a woman should ever refuse an offer of marriage."

– Pride and Prejudice

So much love and eloquence

Staging 'Persuasion'

Interview with director Jeff James

In 2017, Jeff James wrote and directed an adaptation of *Persuasion* for Manchester Royal Exchange Theatre.

How did you decide on the kind of adaptation you wanted to make of Austen's work?

Well, I came to the novel thinking it might be an interesting thing to put on stage. I didn't know Jane Austen that well. I think I'd read *Pride and Prejudice* and *Emma* in my early twenties, but I hadn't really engaged with her for a while when I first got into *Persuasion*. I wanted to make a theatre production that spoke to our world today. And what really struck me when I read the novel for the first time was how different it seemed to me from those previous chocolate box adaptations. There's a real kind of baggage that her novels have accumulated over the past 200 years that is particularly connected to costume and also to real estate. The movie and TV adaptations of her novels often inflate the characters' wealth so that they seem even posher than they are in her novels.

And reading *Persuasion* I was really struck that the kind of central question for Austen, for her characters, and for Anne Elliot is how do you organize your life? How do you balance the competing demands of money, sex, and family? You have to find a way to navigate that. I was beginning the adaptation in my late twenties, early thirties, when lots of the people around me were getting married, starting to have babies, trying to buy houses, or were stressed about being unable to buy houses. And all of these questions that are very related to each other seemed to be really dominant in *Persuasion*. I think there's a way that Jane Austen's novels have been caricatured, that they prioritize marriage over any other way of living, and that they are preoccupied with the choices that posh girls make regarding who they choose to marry.

But what I found reading the novel was that those choices are not trivial at all – they're life or death. Who you choose to marry or whether you get married or not, or whether you have children or not, have huge ramifications on your happiness, on your wealth, even today and perhaps more today than it did forty years ago. This connects to your life today. In order to suggest that to the audience, I made the choice that everything in the production that you could see would look like it was from the 21st century.

It was really important to me to have a diverse cast of actors and to centre non-white actors in the show. So Anne was played by a Black woman, and that seemed to me really important for making the characters look like the people in our world today. Often Austen's stories have been staged or filmed with an all-white cast. This was all before *Bridgerton*, which was another important step, I think, in showing that these Regency stories could have non-white actors. That seemed to me like a really important political choice to make it clear that these stories were not only for one group of people in our society and that the show reflected and represented our world today.

As I was creating the adaptation with the dramaturg James Yeatman, I was very aware that some people had successfully relocated Austen stories to the late 20th century. For me, the most successful adaptation that does that is *Clueless*. I thought a lot about whether I should do that, about whether the characters should be living in the 21st century. But I thought it was more interesting for my adaptation for there to be a jostle between the early 19th century and the early 21st century, and that the production existed across both those moments in history. So the rules of the production were that everything you see is from the 21st century, but everything that the characters say is as if they are living in the early 19th century. So they still talk about the Navy, they still talk about carriages, they don't have mobile phones, so it's not actually located in the 21st century, but everything you see is 21st century. And I think that approach forced the audience to encounter the story as something that speaks to us today.

So you presented two parallel moments in time which encouraged the audience to examine now and then?

Exactly. And they were in tension with each other sometimes. For example, the play starts with a joke where Mrs Clay is dancing to this song, *Call Your Girlfriend* by Robin, a song from 2010. And then Elizabeth comes onto the stage and says, "Be quiet, Penelope, I can hardly hear myself think over the sound of your harpsichord." So at the very beginning of the show, there's this joke that in some ways we are using 21st century music, and the music is a really key element of this production to express what's going on for these characters, but the characters themselves are able to interpret it through an early 19th century lens.

Had you seen any other productions done in this way?

I was working a lot at that time with the director Ivo van Hove, and his work had certainly influenced me. For example, his production *Roman Tragedies* uses Shakespeare's text, but locates it in a 21st century political world. But I think what I was trying to do with Alex Lowde, who designed it, was create something really specific to deliver this story and to deliver that world of *Persuasion*. And one choice that became really central to the audience's experience and to the success of the production was thinking about how to dramatize and express the trip to the seaside when they go to Lyme Regis, which is at the midpoint of the novel.

For Austen I think the seaside always kind of equals sexuality, and we had this idea that the characters should be in swimming costumes of some kind at that point. And

Staging 'Persuasion'

basically, we had this idea that Lyme Regis should be a kind of foam party, so we ended up spraying hundreds of gallons of foam onto the stage every night, which was technically quite demanding for the theatres where we produced this, but I think this was a really useful kind of explosion of chaos at the centre of the show. It's at that point when they go to Lyme Regis that Wentworth and Louisa's romance is at its high point.

Anne is seeing the kind of fun she could be having if she was able to be more daring or be braver in some way or if she hadn't rejected Wentworth eight years previously. That foam party was a really fun part of the show, and I really like stage elements that change how the actors can move on stage. I've put on productions using lots of treacle, I've had productions using hundreds of footballs, and this sense of mess and chaos

Caroline Maroney as Henriette, Helen Cripps as Mary, Fred Fergus as Wentworth and Matilda Bailes as Louisa. Photo: Andy Paradise

on stage I really enjoy. I think that really came from the novel, and it was really useful that at that point in the production, it's the only time when only the young people are present. We came to the idea of the foam party through the idea of Club 18–30, Ibiza kind of hijinks, and that staging idea really unlocked the emotion at that point in the story.

Can you talk about the decisions that went into choosing the set?

When we first made this show it was at the Royal Exchange in Manchester, so it was in the round and the audience were all the way around the stage. We wanted to find a way to create a focus at the centre of that. The rectangular plinth felt really useful as a way to create a focus there. We wanted to give the audience different perspectives at different times in the show and not to privilege any particular viewpoint on that. It's a kind of seven-sided shape, I think, at the Exchange.

And we found a kind of psychological track through the show that every time Anne and Wentworth reencountered each other, the plinth would turn. So at the beginning of the show, the plinth was just this kind of rectangle to show that when Anne is in Kellynch, it's a place where all of the sexual possibilities have run out, there's no one left to marry anyone. There aren't any possibilities for the next generation.

So in that part of the show, the plinth is just a rectangular block, and it's only when Anne goes to Uppercross where Charles and Mary live and she meets Wentworth again that new possibilities open for her. That was a key moment in the show where they meet standing at either ends of the plinth and the plinth turned, opening up new possibilities for her. And then again, the plinth turns when Wentworth comes back into her life. It's kind of a cliché that the world shifts when she sees the love of her life again, but it felt very helpful and it does feel like her world cracks and changes at both of those points. Then the plinth turned a final time at the very end when Anne and Wentworth are reunited and they kiss, and as they're kissing, the plinth turns back to its original position. At this point, the solid rectangle is no longer arid infertility, but kind of harmony and conclusion, I guess.

Can you talk about the use of music? How was that designed in terms of underscoring the emotional story?

I think that the most important music in it, I would say, is the three tracks from Frank Ocean's album, *Channel Orange*. I found that the longing and desire expressed in that album connected really perfectly to where Anne is at during different points of the show, particularly the song 'Thinking About You', which is what plays when she first meets Wentworth. It's just this great song of having not seen someone for a long time, but them still taking up a big space in your brain and having that longing for them that Anne obviously does.

And then the other song on that album that I really love and that I think is really important in the show is 'Lost', which I think is about a lover who is somewhere else, who is traveling around having a glamorous life, but has forgotten the singer of the song and is probably cheating on them. That plays when Wentworth comes back to Bath, and back into Anne's life. One of the big choices we made was that the section in Bath, would be set in a nightclub. So, the space is quite dark and quite closed down. And when Wentworth turns up again, Anne is dancing with Mr Elliot and she has basically given up on Wentworth. I stole a plot device from *Sense and Sensibility* I think, I can't quite remember, that she hears that Wentworth has married, which doesn't quite happen in *Persuasion*. And in fact it's Louisa and Benwick who have got married, but because of that information she thinks, "Well, Wentworth is a dead end," so she decides to go for it with William Elliot. We see her during that song 'Lost' making out with Mr Elliot while Wentworth comes in and sees them. She breaks away from Mr Elliot and sees Wentworth and that's one of the moments when the plinth turns. That song 'Lost' is also really good because it lists all of these glamorous places the person is traveling to such as Tokyo, New York, Los Angeles. So you have this real kind of contemporary sense. These aren't places, obviously, that are named in Jane Austen's novel, but I think having them spoken in the show gives us a sense of the 21st century in a really helpful way.

There was a huge divide between Wentworth's character, having been away and fought in the Napoleonic Wars, and the life that Anne has been living during that time, very sheltered, doing embroidery and domestic duties?

I think it is really important that Wentworth has been transformed over those eight years. It's a slightly rogue idea for Anne to marry him. That's why the novel is called *Persuasion*, because she's persuaded *not* to marry him. She's persuaded it's a bad idea. Then when he comes back eight years later, because of those experiences in the Napoleonic Wars, because of that freedom he was able to enjoy as a man, he's been totally transformed as a prospect. Whereas because of the cruel march of time, Anne is a much less attractive prospect because she's eight years older and therefore in the ideology of the time, eight years less attractive, eight years less fertile. And I think I tried to convey those rules to the audience.

The first scene in my show is Elizabeth receiving a letter that she hopes is going to be a proposal of marriage, when in fact, it's an invitation to the wedding of the person she was hoping was going to ask to marry her. So you see immediately the kind of cruelty of this world and the high stakes of it.

Like Austen, I also tried to dramatize the quite limited possibilities for women. It's so brilliant the way Austen has these very funny characters, Charles and Mary, and Mary has got what the other two sisters want, in a way. She's successfully married someone who's well-off, but she's really miserable and she's raising these young children. Even though she probably doesn't have that much to do with the young children, the strains and stresses of domestic life are not enjoyable for her. The way I dealt with gender was through these specific characters, through their desires and through their problems and trying to dramatize those.

You could say that young women today have got a similar imperative to try and find a mate and have children before the age of 40?

Definitely. That was something I was really thinking about and was aware of. As I say, while lots has changed in the last 200 years, people are still trapped in time and still have to make choices with limited information to guide them, and those choices can make or break their lives. So I think the parallels are much closer than the differences, actually.

And the theme of unrequited love, missing out on the person who's the love of your life, that is still the basis of romcom today, isn't it?

Absolutely. *Persuasion* is structured to have Wentworth present in Anne's life from the very beginning, but we don't quite understand who he was or what he means to her until a little bit later. There aren't that many scenes just between Anne and Wentworth in the novel, or in my show; there were maybe three or four. I think those questions about how you decide whether someone is the right person for you were really revealing about character and identity and about what it is like to be alive. They are much deeper than people give them credit for. Obviously some romcoms are trivial but I do think that romcoms are seen to be favoured by women and therefore they're dismissed, but this is due to patriarchy. I think Austen really shows that those questions are high stakes and absolutely integral to who one is as a person.

What was the audience's reaction to the play?

They really liked it. It was this huge hit and really launched my career as a director. I think whenever I'm making work, I try and make things that appeal to my sensibility and hope that even if I'm a bit of a weirdo, there are enough other weirdos in the world who will be interested in it and engage with it. And definitely with this one, there really were. As we were making it, I remember there were a few people in the Royal Exchange who were anxious about whether the audience would understand it? Would they get what they were expecting? ? But once we had an audience, we all realized it worked both for people who love Austen and for those who think they don't like Austen.

Any plans to bring it back this year because it's the 250th anniversary of Austen's birth?

Oh, I'd love to. I still would love to get it into the West End. I think it's a show with big popular appeal, and maybe if we could get the right casting in there that would make that possible. I'm also talking to a theatre in Latvia about doing it there, so I imagine I haven't seen the last of it, and I'm glad about that because I love the show a lot.

In terms of Jane Austen as a writer, what do you think the legacy is of her work today?

I think her influence is measureless, really, isn't it? I mean, she basically invented free indirect style in English and found this way of getting inside characters' heads more successfully than any novelist before her. And the sophistication of that style was one of the things that I found so hard to crack. That so much of what she's doing for the reader is about the interior world of her characters, particularly of Anne Elliot in *Persuasion*. One of the challenges in staging it was that so much of what Anne does, particularly in the very first part of the novel, is just watching people. So finding ways to express what's going on for Anne was a challenge. One of the ways I did that was to have this expressionistic device that she would

Staging 'Persuasion'

show her frustration to the audience in a way that she couldn't show it to the people around her. So she would basically throw the other characters off the plinth and there were crash mats so they would just bounce straight back.

That allowed me to make her kind of an active element in those first few scenes where in the novel she's just watching. But I think what Austen achieved in the six major novels is unparalleled. The architecture of those novels and the way they are so formidably structured is one of the things I really admire about them.

I think she taught Henry James a lot, in terms of that very structured and architectural way of writing a novel. But unlike Henry James, you don't see the architecture as much because it's so sensitively done. I think that allows her to give readers an insight into what it is like to know another human being, to fall in love with them, to choose a life with them. I think because of that sensitivity, she will be read forever.

What about the ending of your play? Did it differ from the book at all?

One thing I didn't know how to do for ages was the letter that Wentworth writes to Anne, because letters are really boring on stage. You can't have someone just standing there reading a letter. And I also thought that it was probably non-negotiable, the letter; it's so beautiful, it's so beautifully written.

One of the things at the heart of the novel is choosing whether or not to get married, but also choosing whether or not to have children and how connected those choices were then. They are less so now. It was important for me that the audience could see those children. So the child of Mary and Charles who falls out of a tree and has this accident in the Uppercross section, we had a child actor who was about six or seven playing him, and I wanted him to come back at the end of the story, partly to remind the audience that this is probably where Anne and Wentworth are heading. And during that conversation between Admiral and Mrs Croft and Anne, Captain Wentworth was just sat watching them on the other side of the plinth. I didn't have any props in the show really so he couldn't have a pen or anything to write a letter. As a kind of *deus ex machina*, the little boy ran in at the end of that conversation with a letter and said, "Captain Wentworth has written you a letter."

Then Admiral and Mrs Croft left while Anne read out the letter so we could hear the words. That was one of the times in the show when I was most closely using Austen's text. It was quite long that letter, so I didn't use all of it, but I did basically use that text. When I was first starting the adaptation, partly out of laziness, I was hoping that I could mainly use the text she'd written. But I found when I was working with actors doing R&D on the play, that if you read out the dialogue that Austen had written, you just sound like a mad person. It is much more complex and convoluted than ordinary human speech. So what I was trying to do in the show was to write a text that, to the audience, sounded like it was lifted from the novel, but it rarely was. Probably a third of the playtext is taken from the novel, but most of it is not.

I wanted in that final moment to give this sense of resolution and a sense of the future that Anne and Wentworth are looking towards. So that's why the little boy came in.

Staging 'Persuasion'

Jeff James is a theatre director and writer. Jeff's credits as both writer and director include *Winter's Tale* (Dailes Theatre, Riga), *Persuasion* (Manchester Royal Exchange, and later revived at Rose Theatre Kingston, Alexandra Palace Theatre and Oxford Playhouse), *Noah and the Peacock* (Nottingham Playhouse on Zoom), and *Stink Foot* (The Yard Theatre). His credits as director include: *Shooting Hedda Gabler* (Rose Theatre Kingston), *First Touch* (Nottingham Playhouse), *La Musica* (Young Vic), *One for the Road/Victoria Station* (Young Vic and Print Room). His credits as dramaturg include *Coppélia* (Scottish Ballet, Edinburgh International Festival and Sadler's Wells) and *Richard II* (Almeida). Jeff has worked as associate director on seven of Ivo van Hove's productions, including *A View from the Bridge* (Young Vic, West End and Broadway) and *A Little Life* (West End). www.jeffwjames.com

The arrival of the Gardiners

Meeting with Jane

April de Angelis

Jane enters.

APRIL: Jane, I don't know how to tell you this, but you'd better sit down.

Jane sits.

You're incredibly famous.
One of the most famous people who's ever lived.
The most famous novelist ever.
You're on a banknote.
People dress like you and have tea parties. You have your own society.
You're studied in universities across the world.
You've spawned an industry, academic and cultural.
On your frail shoulders rests an empire.
(Benign, unlike the one you took a dig at in *Mansfield Park*).
People go on pilgrimages to Chawton.
One can do Jane Austen walks in Bath.
Bath is famous because of you. That place you stood against a wall watching society reproduce around you and feeling like a stale seed. Now they are selling mugs, cushions and small bags of lavender with tasteful bows, impressed with your face.
You said *Pride and Prejudice* was your baby. Well, that baby matured into the novel by which every other must be judged for eternity. I know. Just sit there and take that in.

Encounters with Jane Austen

Jane does.

Every woman who ever read *P&P* lusts after Darcy. You wrote the perfect man. Of course, it spoilt real men for us ever after, but we don't hold that against you because Darcy is worth it.

And we have Elizabeth. As you put it "as delightful a creature" that ever appeared in print. The second of five sisters with an "estate entailed away from the female line" she braved the world armed only with a bright mind, bright eyes and a gloriously able tongue but nonetheless got everything, especially Darcy. Unbelievably, we don't hold that against her. We love that she did because she is *us*. The best us we can imagine. Us in our *dreaming*.

The list of your characters is nothing short of miraculous. They are household names! As if they were old friends but ones picked out in your especial light, glinting and gleaming. Emma, the gorgeously self-deluding heroine who can only approach her desire for Knightley through a cypher, Miss Harriet Smith, perfectly distanced by class and wetness. The quiet heroism of reduced circumstances and paltry social cachet of the older unmarried woman, the hysterically garrulous Miss Bates punctured with Emma's breathtaking spike of cruelty on that picnic. And my particular favourite, the ingenue now 'stale' at 27, having missed the boat (and its captain), Anne Elliot. Relegated to almost governess, how her youthful mistake, to be persuaded against her better judgement to follow snobbish advice rather than meaningful connection, impales her endlessly with unspeakable regret as the monsters around her are happily buoyed by money and position in a society that can't recognise real worth and spirit. And the final joy of reconciliation with her lover.

Meeting with Jane

When Frederick Wentworth announces he will marry Anne, her father responds with the immortal line "Anne, whatever for?" Will Anne sail away with Frederick? Leave the confining world of teacups, hypocrisy and calling cards? Brave the wild and open sea? We hope so. Like the small girl in *Sense and Sensibility* hiding under the table, carving out an oasis of self-determining space, pouring over an atlas, dreaming of freedom of adventure. Female desire is there but you have to look for it.

Did I see your eyes flicker? Your expression is inscrutable.

And then there are the men. Armed only with a pen you tear them to shreds.

Jane's right eyebrow lifts imperceptibly.

Let's start with Mr Collins. He's so awful he's not even got the chutzpah to be bad. Just a self-important, mansplainer clown without a sliver of redeeming self-knowledge, a man who can never laugh at himself. Oh yes, a type still in plentiful supply. How you stuck the knife, so brazenly yet with surgical precision, into the overinflated, unearned power and entitlement of male pomposity and brought forth not blood but deliciously subversive laughter. Jane, we have so much to thank you for, you don't know the half! How can you just sit there unmoving, staring with your seriously mysterious brown eyes? Your paisley sprigged dress unruffled?

Jane sits, inscrutable.

Let me add a few more since I've got you here. There's the weak Willoughby, Mr Elton, the sex pest, the paedophile, Wickham, the plausible but disingenuous Mr William Elliot on the hunt for land/money and prepared to feign love to do it, the buffoonish brother in *Sense and Sensibility* and his self-serving wife, who cruelly neglect a mother and her daughters after the death of the family

Encounters with Jane Austen

patriarch (something you had bitter experience of), even the prideful Darcy before his lesson — all of them primed through callousness, insensitivity and their own self-serving needs to be wrecking balls to the lives of women. You let none of them off the hook. You didn't like the King much, either, did you? You took the side of the philandering George IV's estranged wife "because she is a woman and because I hate her husband." Strong words about the most powerful man in the land. But what had you got to lose that they hadn't taken from you already? Education, property, position? From the edges you blasted the centre, disguised in the most sparkling prose and greatest storytelling the novel can boast.

Jane's right hand moves very slightly.

Your humour, fresh as the day it was born, wickedly astute, pinions the pretensions of misguided self-importance: Lady Catherine de Bourgh and her barouche box, Mr Collins' ghastly mixture of "pomposity and servility". His hilarious admonition to Lizzie, "It is by no means certain that another offer of marriage may ever be made to you." Surely, the least inducement any man could have uttered? Austenian irony at its sharpest.

"I wish we had a Donkey," opines Mrs Elton in *Emma*. And we giggle at her inflated social aspirations resting on the back of this humble animal.

Women writers were a rarity. How did you ever find the self-belief to think that you were one?
Did it come to you on a walk one fine spring morning? Was it a revelation on a brooding autumn afternoon? Perhaps stories began to brew in you from childhood or did it happen in the heady but agonising secret life of adolescence?

You prefer to keep that to yourself?

Jane does.

Meeting with Jane

Did you get a real kick out of reading your fragments to your family? We know you did that.

You thought of your novels as your children. You made the bold move to mother them instead of taking your wifely place amongst the goods and chattels of a Mr X? You thought big and outside the box, creating a mental life with roots in the few women authors out there – Burney and Edgeworth.

Those roots/routes you chose flowering to extraordinary fruition in those six wondrous books. Yes, that's all we have of you. So little and so much.

A curl escapes from beneath Jane's cap.

I haven't even started on the movies.
The TV adaptations, the plays.

It's quite hard to explain because I'd have to explain electricity, cameras and the moving image. Television! Just take it from me, your stories are beamed into everyone's home. And the love, the *love*. It's hardest to explain the *love*. Bordering on obsession. Worship. Adoration. Your stories are miracles. Your face in that curiously unflattering sketch by Cassandra with your eyes aslant haunts us with a desire for more.

We would devour you if we could, we love you that much.

You pose a mighty question: how could a young woman, so hidden away, so overlooked, wield her pen with such devastating wit, social and psychological acumen, such power as to overcome the world forever?

You say nothing. You never did. Just one passing reference to what a novelist needs, "just four families in a neighborhood." I paraphrase. You make it sound easy. Was it easy for you? Did it bring you dark nights of the soul? Did you doubt? Throw down your pen and nib? But they would never have

Encounters with Jane Austen

brought you your modest, wee, writing-desk box if
you were a doubter. You came from thrifty folk.
I knew you wouldn't answer.
Cassandra's picture shows a determined clamp of the lip.
The sideways glance, a refusal to give up secrets easily.
Well, I tried. We will have to guess.
As you yourself said – you don't write for dull elves.

I take my leave. But can I just say – Jane, you were
glorious. Your books were/are/and shall be forever.
They are one of the things that make life worth living.
Thank you. I hope you knew, somewhere with the
same guiding intuition, that same uncanny genius,
that you would one day be everyone's Jane Austen.
Jane exits.

Sketch portrait of Jane Austen aged 35, in
watercolour and pencil by Cassandra Austen c.1810
Image courtesy of NPG

Meeting with Jane

April De Angelis is an acclaimed writer whose extensive theatre work includes; *The Divine Mrs S* (Hampstead Theatre); *Infamous* (Jermyn Street Theatre); *Kerry Jackson* (National Theatre); *Saving Grace* (Riverside Studios); *Gin Craze!* (Royal & Derngate Theatre); *My Brilliant Friend*, A Two Part Dramatization Of Elena Ferrantes' Epic Family Saga (Rose Theatre Kingston, National Theatre); *The Village* (Theatre Royal Stratford East, 2018); *Frankenstein* (Royal Exchange Manchester, 2018 *Gastronauts* (Royal Court Upstairs, 2013); *Jumpy* (Royal Court 2011 & Duke Of York's Theatre 2012, Melbourne And Sydney 2015); An Adaptation of *Wuthering Heights* (Birmingham Rep, 2008); *Wild East* (Royal Court 2006, Young Vic 2019); *A Laughing Matter* (Out of Joint At National Theatre, 2001); *A Warwickshire Testimony* (RSC, 1999); *The Positive Hour* (Out of Joint At Hampstead Theatre, 1997); *Playhouse Creatures* (Sphinx Theatre Company At The Haymarket Theatre 1993 And Revived At The Old Vic Theatre, 1997 and again at Chichester Festival Theatre In 2013); *The Life And Times Of Fanny Hill* (The Old Fire Station Oxford, 1991; revived at The Bristol Old Vic, 2015) And *Flight* (Glyndebourne Opera, 1997).

Photo: Andy Woods

She has contributed the play *Crux* to *Seven Plays by Women* (1991); 'Jenny' to *The Women Writers' Handbook* ed Anne Sandham (2020) and 'How Feminism has influenced my Playwriting' to *Feminist Theatre Then and Now* (2024) all published by Aurora Metro/Supernova Books.

Before she could reply to the entreaties of several that she would sing again, she was eagerly succeeded at the instrument by her sister Mary.

"Without music life would be a blank for me."

– Emma

She played and sang: Jane Austen and Music

Gillian Dooley & Jennie Batchelor

at York Festival of Ideas.[1]

Jennie: Today we will be discussing Gillian Dooley's latest book, *She Played and Sang: Jane Austen and Music*. This is a book that's so rich in detail, it's so rich in detective work, and you say in your introduction that it's the product of a lifetime of thinking about music in Austen's novels. So how did you come to research *She Played and Sang*?

Gillian: It started with reading *Pride and Prejudice* in high school and noticing that Mary and Elizabeth Bennet were both musicians, but they were different types of musicians, and that Elizabeth, though not playing half so well, was listened to with much more pleasure. I thought that was an interesting thing to say. I still think it's an interesting thing to say. I'm not quite sure what it means. But I like to try and unpack these little side remarks that she makes about music.

Jennie: So from reading *Pride and Prejudice*, where did you go from there? I think many of us are struck by those little moments in the novel, but how did those interests snowball to enable you to write this book many years later?

Gillian: My Honours thesis was on music in Austen's novels, and that set me off on the trail. Another 10 years later I discovered the music collection, which I didn't really know about in detail before. Some catalogues of the music collection

---

[1] edited and abridged transcript from online session 2024. The full interview is available on the York Festival of Ideas YouTube Channel.

She played and sang: Jane Austen and Music

had been published by then, so I could find out what was in the music collection. As I'm also an amateur musician I could put together programs of the music, so with some colleagues at Flinders University I was able to put together the first 'Jane Austen's Music' concert of readings and songs in 2007, and it just seemed like too good a thing to stop doing it, so I've kept doing it ever since.

Jennie: I'm fascinated by that journey. It starts from a moment in the novel and it expands out to other of the Austen novels, and it spills out into her life and those collections and the catalogues. But thinking about the life, one of the things that struck me – one of the things we know – is that Austen didn't have very much by way of formal education. What have you been able to piece together about her education in music and how important music was to her life?

Gillian: As with much of her early life, there are little clues and people have built big assumptions on those clues. One is in a letter to Cassandra from 1796 when she mentioned Mr Chard and said that she would practise the piano harder to make him feel better, but that's the only time she mentions him and there are no accounts that say he's been paid to be her music teacher or anything. It's just assumed from that that he was her music teacher and had been for 10 years. There is a vague memory from her niece Anna, that she thought somebody came from Winchester to teach the piano but she wasn't sure. One thing that we do have, though, is two albums of manuscript sheet music that belong to Ann Cawley. Jane and Cassandra were sent to Oxford in 1783 to be taught by Mrs Cawley, who was her mother's brother-in-law's sister. She didn't have a school: she just took Cassandra and Jane, and Jane Cooper, their cousin, to be students. That didn't last long for various reasons, but somehow those music books that belonged to Ann, that she had had in the 1750s, came into the Austen family music collection and presumably did belong at some stage to Jane herself. So obviously, music education was included, which would have been a normal part of a girl's education. They would all have learned some rudiments of music. Whether it 'took' or not is another matter.

Jennie: How did it 'take' with Jane Austen? What can we piece together?

Gillian: It seems that she kept on with it. She wanted to have a piano. She spent her money on hiring a piano when they were in Southampton. She was the one who said, yes we will have a piano, when they moved to Chawton. Her niece Caroline, James's younger daughter, is probably the best source we have for Jane Austen's musical activity, even though she was only 12 when Jane died. Caroline had memories that she recounted more than 50 years later. She can even remember the songs that she sang in her last years, and that sort of testimony is some of the most precious material that we have about Austen's music.

Jennie: I want to ask a little bit more about the music books you've mentioned, including Ann Cawley's books. You make really extensive and ingenious use of the Austen family music collection throughout *She Played and Sang*. This is a collection of print and manuscript books that were owned by members of the Austen family, four of which, I seem to remember, have at least some music that is in Austen's own hand. The books are available online at Internet Archive, if readers want to delve into this a little more.

Could you tell us a little more about the music books that you discuss in *She Played and Sang* – who they belonged to, and what kind of insights they give us into the role of music in Austen's life and in the Austen family more generally?

Gillian: Firstly, there are Ann Cawley's two music books. They had pieces by Handel in them, and some of the older composers. Then there are music books that belonged to her cousin, Eliza Hancock, who married the French count and later married Henry Austen after the count died. There's

She played and sang: Jane Austen and Music

a lot of French music from that part of the collection, and there's some print music in that collection which Jane copied into her own music book, so you can see that they had a musical friendship, even though Eliza was fourteen years older than Jane. There are some pieces of French music that weren't readily available in England in Jane's own manuscript collection, so we can assume that at least some of it probably came via Eliza.

Then there was music that belonged to her brother Edward's wife, Elizabeth. It's all females who had these collections. I don't know if men had music collections, but that's another whole interesting question – the gender divide.

So we have Elizabeth and Eliza – not to be confused – and there's some music in albums that belonged to some of Elizabeth and Edward's daughters, and some of them were actually created, or filled in, after Jane Austen died. In a way they are irrelevant to her own music life, but they are relevant to the musical life of the family and I think they are still interesting.

And then there are the books that belonged to her in some sense. Three of them are almost completely manuscript, mostly in her own handwriting. And then there's a sort of scrapbook which has been rebound and is a mixture of print and manuscript. It has fallen apart and been rebound quite recently.

The books show us a pattern of exchange among the family members. For example, there are some pieces of music in Jane Austen's handwriting in one of Elizabeth's manuscript books. And it's probably because she was staying at Godmersham and did some copying for Elizabeth while she was busy doing something else.

We don't know whether Jane suggested to Elizabeth that she copy a song she herself liked into Elizabeth's book as a way of sharing it, or whether Elizabeth asked Jane to copy something in particular that she wanted to keep from a book on loan from the circulating library, or borrowed from someone.

Jennie: The selection of what gets copied is fascinating. We have an idea about the kind of soundtrack to Jane Austen's life, which we get from music history, or we get from TV and adaptations and so forth, but you say in the book, "The music Jane Austen knew was largely different from the repertoire that a musician of our time usually learns". Could you say a little more about the other kinds of music and composers that we find in the music books, and draw our attention to any kinds of music that our audience might find surprising.

Gillian: I should explain that I catalogued the music myself for the Southampton Library Catalogue a few years ago. Once I had catalogued everything individually, then I made a list and did some analysis of how much of various types of music was in the collection. How much theatre music, or French music, or Scottish music, for example.

There are quite a lot of Scottish folk songs, and themes and variations on Scottish folk songs: so-called Scottish music was very popular – it's a catch-all term. And then Irish music came along too in the early 19th century, thanks to Thomas Moore and his *Irish Melodies*.

There are many songs about sailors and the sea as well, and that was fascinating. Charles Dibdin seems to have been one of her favourite composers. There are a lot of songs by Dibdin in the collection. He is the sort of respectable side of maritime music at the time, but the Dibdin songs are still not ladylike and genteel. They are often in dialect and they're quite forthright in some of their opinions and expressions, with cursing and so on, and they're very funny. And you can see the sort of humour that's in those songs is reflected in Austen's Juvenilia – or at least you can see that she would have appreciated that humour.

She played and sang: Jane Austen and Music

Then there are the German drinking songs. Who expected to find German drinking songs in Jane Austen's collection?

Jennie: I'm wondering what that kind of discovery does to your sense of Jane Austen. There are the French examples too. They are all pretty arresting in different ways. Did it change your sense of Jane Austen?

Gillian: The more I've learnt about her, the more I'm expecting to be surprised. You read the letters and the Juvenilia – and her sense of humour! She doesn't always necessarily allow that to come through quite in the same way in the published novels, but she was a very witty woman. But she wasn't just flippant, she was incredibly intelligent. She made a joke about being ignorant and uneducated, but she wasn't. She was very well read.

Another thing, as you say, is the French music – not just the French songs per se but songs about the French Revolution. There are anti-revolutionary songs, and the 'Marseillaise', with all the verses written out in French, alongside the ballad telling the story of Marie Antoinette and how terrible it is that she's been imprisoned.

Jennie: That's such an extraordinary juxtaposition. It raises so many interesting questions, not just about Jane Austen's wit and her intelligence, but I wonder how much it helps – or doesn't help – in fathoming her politics. It certainly shows how well versed she was in events beyond the place she happened to be living at the time, which was rural Hampshire, but particularly thinking about that example of the Marie Antoinette ballads and the 'Marseillaise', what kind of sense does that give you of her understanding of and views on the French Revolution?

Gillian: I think she was an observer, she was not a fanatic either way. Obviously when it touched her personally – presumably when the news came of the Comte de Feuillide's execution it must have been very shocking for the family.

But she was aware of these songs. She performed them and knew them and understood their drama. I think it's the

Encounters with Jane Austen

drama of it that puts the Jane Austen that I know in touch with this very dramatic and theatrical material. There are also many songs from the theatre, from operas – not usually Italian operas but arias from operas that have been adapted for English theatre – theatrical music. When you sing them, you're acting a part and you're becoming that person. You're doing what a novelist does.

Jennie: Yes, absolutely. I'll come back to the point about composing and writing novels and music, in a moment. But maybe we should turn to the novels at this point. One of the things you draw our attention to in the book is that there's famously very little specific detail about individual pieces of music or individual composers in the novels – Robin Adair in *Emma*. But there are so many musical instruments – pianos figure quite prominently in many of the novels, and singing; performances appear in the novels, there are lyrics strewn in various places. How does music work in the novels, what kind of role does music play in the fiction?

Gillian: When I wrote that Honours thesis on music in the novels in 1995 I thought there was no point in looking at *Northanger Abbey* because there's no music in that novel. But I was recently asked to write a chapter on *Northanger Abbey* so I thought I'd better look again. I found that there's not very much but it does refer back to music in the Gothic novel. And in the scene where John Thorpe thinks he's proposing to Catherine and she doesn't notice, he hums a tune. Why does he hum a tune? It's about the only appealing thing he ever does.

Jennie: I suppose it depends on his humming, really. Knowing John Thorpe I don't have particularly high expectations for the calibre of his music.

Gillian: True! But Henry Tilney mentions music in passing a few times, and there's a broken lute in the fantasy Gothic castle that he describes to Catherine, which is straight out of *The Mysteries of Udolpho*.

She played and sang: Jane Austen and Music

But once we get to *Sense and Sensibility*, Marianne is musical to the core and shares music with Willoughby. The contrast between Marianne, the musical one, and Elinor, the non-musical one, is evident. There often is a pair like that in the novels. But they are all such different characters. You've got Elinor and Marianne, and then you've got Jane and Elizabeth Bennet: Jane's not musical but Elizabeth is, but they are completely different people from Elinor and Marianne, and Fanny Price and Mary Crawford in *Mansfield Park* again are quite different people. So Austen uses music but she doesn't use it in any kind of schematic way. Their musicianship or lack of interest is part of the person, the character, who they are. You can't put a template over it.

You can a little bit with the men, though. There are very few musical men in Austen who are the ones you'd want to marry. They're the unreliable ones – the Frank Churchills, the Willoughbys ...

The whole thing about music and masculinity in England is quite an interesting study in itself, actually.

Jennie: Yes, especially putting that in conjunction with what you said earlier about none of the music books belonging to men. I'm struck by what you said; there's not a template, there's not a schematic way of understanding music in Austen. I always feel with Austen nothing is mentioned without having some kind of significance beyond itself. So if there's a piano in a novel, or a harp, as is the case with Mary Crawford, it's telling us a story and it might tell us a different story in a different novel. It would be rather easy to fall into a trap of just thinking that music is the soundtrack of ordinary life so of course there's music in the novels, but one of the things that your book shows is that it's absolutely not the kind of wallpaper to the novels. It's doing interesting and different things in each one of the novels.

Gillian: I often hear people saying that all young women were supposed to be accomplished and it's something they had to do to catch a husband. I think that's not true. If they had an education they were probably given a chance to learn music. If they liked it they might have persisted with it. Some of them might have done it to try and make an impression. But people were people. They weren't all little automatons. And they certainly didn't all conform to the rules in the etiquette books. The etiquette books were there to try to control behaviour that was happening. They weren't there to describe behaviour that was actually happening.

Jennie: No, there wouldn't have been quite so many if people had been behaving themselves.

One of the things that we haven't touched on yet is about musicianship and writing. Could you say more about the relationship you see between Austen's writing style and music and how we might think of writing as analogous to music or composing in some form?

Gillian: In a way, it's one of those things that's hard to pin down. When you read her prose aloud it's such a delight, and it's a little bit like singing. It has a rhythm, and the sentences have form, and they land in a certain way. It is very much the rhetoric of the 18th century but it's also something she has refined herself, that she has brought alive. She was a singer and a pianist. Why would that not feed into her prose? Of course, reading aloud was something they did all the time. She read her own novels aloud to the family.

Jennie: That sort of performance – the way performance connects the writing and musicianship – I think that's something we often forget as modern readers of Jane Austen, the sociable reading, reading in the household, reading aloud, listening to somebody else reading, or as we know from the Austen family the sort of private theatricals they engaged in – these activities were very much part and parcel of lives at the time, while we tend to sit there reading them quietly

She played and sang: Jane Austen and Music

in our heads. It's a very modern way of thinking about what reading is. At the time reading was much more like a musical performance, and it was heard and received in a slightly different way.

Gillian: There are many descriptions of reading things aloud in the letters. There's also this myth about the squeaky hinge and how she'd hide her manuscript away if someone opened the door. She didn't want to be named on her title pages. That didn't mean that she didn't want anyone else to know that she was writing. I think it was a matter of taste and habit.

Jennie: Anonymised publication was so normalised in that period. No one calls Daniel Defoe demure, but all of his stuff was published anonymously.

Gillian: We should start a new trend, I think. Demure Defoe.

Jennie: We have a question from a listener: Is there any indication what kind of music Jane Austen preferred? (45:45)

Gillian: One thing that's different is that we think of the musical canon as being anything from the last 500 years or more. We all know music that was written in the 17th and 18th and 19th centuries. She hardly knew any music that was written before about 1750. Most of the composers she had among her music collection were her contemporaries. When we think of contemporary classical music now, it's quite a niche thing to go to a new music concert, but then it was very much the music that was coming out at the time that she seems to have sought out. She certainly had several pieces of music by Haydn. He's one of the few canonical composers that she actually knew about. She had a little bit of Mozart in her collection but it wasn't actually named as Mozart. There are the comic songs by Charles Dibdin. There are a lot of very beautiful love songs. There are songs by James Hook and Samuel Webbe and Samuel Arnold, some Irish songs and lot of Scottish songs. There are some French songs by François Devienne and Grétry, and Paisiello, the Italian composer. Songs that have drama and feeling. Also a lot of piano music by Pleyel, Clementi, Stamitz, Dussek – composers who we do hear of nowadays occasionally.

Jennie: Yes, I was struck by the eclecticism of her musical taste as reflected in the music books. We have another question. In a lot of Austen's novels there are moments when we can say music is implied, though she never specifically acknowledges it, at parties and balls, so why do you think she chooses to bring the reader's attention to certain instances of music and not others. Is she aiming at what we would think of as cinematic?

Gillian: That's a really interesting question. She would have thought of it as theatrical, I suppose. She was a very discriminating theatregoer. She would go to the theatre and see the latest star, and she would come out saying the music was ok, but she was usually disappointed. The other thing is that music had to have someone playing it or singing it at the time. There was no music otherwise. She doesn't need to describe the music when there's a ball. Musical specifics are telling something about the characters or providing a scenario for something to happen. In the wonderful scene at the Coles' party in *Emma*, there's so much going on which is to do with music. Jane is singing and her voice is getting tired, and Emma is watching Mr Knightley watching Jane singing, and so on. It's such amazing scene-setting. I'm not sure that it's a cinematic effect. I think of it more as a subjective experience through the point of the view of the character – what the character is noticing and what the character is screening out.

Jennie: It does chime so nicely with what you said earlier about drama. Drama is never far from music in Austen's novels. And as you say, she seems drawn in her music books to music that has dramatic qualities of different kinds. One more question: You spoke a bit about different instruments in Austen's novels, like Mary Crawford playing the harp rather than the piano forte. And I wonder what your thoughts are

She played and sang: Jane Austen and Music

about how this might reflect those characters and their traits and morality. I guess it ties in a bit with what you've just been saying – different instruments and what they say about the characters who play them.

Gillian: The piano was the modern instrument in the 1780s and 1790s, taking over from the harpsichord, and then the harp became fashionable, particularly in France, and then it came over to England in the 1790s and the early 1800s. These large harps – pedal harps and lever harps, not the smaller folk harps – were much more expensive than pianos at the time. They were very modern and were a sign of wealth. Mary Crawford in *Mansfield Park* has a harp, the Musgrove sisters in *Persuasion* have a harp between them. Whereas Anne Elliot is a pianist, and I think that the Bertram sisters in *Mansfield Park* play the piano, not the harp. So there is a certain status or income implication there. But the women are never portrayed playing violins or flutes or any of the really portable instruments. And that's significant because of the way it reflects the difficulty that women had getting from A to B.

Jennie: There is a lot more to say but you've given us so much, Gillian, and I just want to thank you for joining us today.

Gillian Dooley is an Honorary Associate Professor in English literature at Flinders University, South Australia. She enjoys researching links between music and literature and bringing them to life in performance. Her interests over 30 years have included novelists Jane Austen, Iris Murdoch, V.S. Naipaul, and J.M. Coetzee, and maritime explorer Matthew Flinders, and she has published widely on their work. Her book She Played and Sang: Jane Austen and Music was published in March 2024.

Jane Austen's Music sites.google.com/site/janeaustensmusic/home

In conversation with the ladies

"Life seems but a quick succession of busy nothings."

– Mansfield Park

A Slow-burn Love Story

Katie Lumsden

I read my first Jane Austen book when I was thirteen years old. It was, predictably, *Pride and Prejudice*, and I liked it, but I did not love it – yet. It did not wow me – yet.

Jane Austen and I have been on a long journey together over the years, and she has gradually changed from one of a number of authors whom I enjoy to an absolute favourite. *Pride and Prejudice* is now the novel I have read the most times, and Jane Austen is certainly the author about whose life I know the most. With other favourite classic authors, I often avoid learning too much about their lives (looking at you, Charles Dickens), but with Jane Austen, the opposite is true. I think I've read more biographies of Austen than I have of all other authors put together.

I first fell in love with nineteenth-century literature as a teenager. It began with *Jane Eyre*, and I was soon working my way through every classic book I could find. I'd soon read all of Austen's novels: *Pride and Prejudice* had been a joy, but I struggled with *Sense and Sensibility*, and *Mansfield Park* dragged. I thought her books too light, too surface level in comparison to the works of Charles Dickens, Thomas Hardy or the Brontës. I was after grit, and I was too young to see it beneath the shimmering surfaces of Jane Austen's novels.

Encountering her work in an academic setting was the first thing to change that. I studied *Pride and Prejudice* at A level and *Mansfield Park* in my first year at university, and both experiences shifted how I thought about Austen. I started to see some of the subtle ways in which she works:

A Slow-burn Love Story

the light-touch social criticism, the universal themes, the clever character portraits. *Mansfield Park* was part of a module on the development of the novel over time, and seeing what an innovative writer Jane Austen was, how new her literary techniques and methods of character development were, made me see her work in a new light. *Mansfield Park* stopped being slow and became fascinating.

The way we read famous authors – especially on a first approach – can be very influenced by the cultural context and expectations around them. Jane Austen is known as a writer of great love stories, and so, as a teenager, I went to all of her books looking for just that. But while some of her novels – *Pride and Prejudice* and *Persuasion* especially – *are* great love stories, they are also multifaceted, and in many, the focus lies elsewhere. If you read *Mansfield Park* as a love story, it's not that exciting. If you read it as a coming-of-age story and a social critique, it becomes something different. I fell in love with *Mansfield Park* at university, and it remains one of my most-loved novels. Fanny Price is probably my favourite Austen heroine; she may not be as witty or charming as Elizabeth Bennet, but she has a quiet inner strength and a firm sense of self.

Nonetheless, Austen didn't really become a favourite author of mine until a few years later, when I found myself living in Bath, studying for an MA in Creative Writing, and working at the Jane Austen Centre. In this part-time role, my job was simple: every weekend, I spent my time dressed in Regency gear, bonnet and all, talking to people about Jane Austen: her work, her life, and why we love her novels.

I worked there for just under a year, and it transformed my relationship with Jane Austen. I learnt about her life, her career and her family for the first time, reading her letters and various biographies. I delved deeper into her work, discovering her hilarious juvenilia, her fascinating unfinished fragments, and her wonderful, too often forgotten epistolary novella *Lady Susan*. When the museum was quiet, the staff were allowed to sit and read, as long as we read Jane Austen – and so I filled my year with her books.

And throughout that time, I was working at a place where everyone loved Austen. The other guides and I would chat about her on our breaks and exchange book recommendations. We never called her 'Austen'; we always called her 'Jane', as though she were a friend. There was (and I believe still is) a wax work of Jane Austen in the final room of the Jane Austen Centre, so I would bid Jane good night every time I closed up the exhibition.

I spent my working days talking to tourists and visitors who loved Jane Austen. I spoke to people from all over the world about why they loved her work, which novel or character was their favourite, which adaptations they thought captured her books the best. I developed ways of recognising the most enthusiastic visitors: each trip to the Jane Austen Centre then began with an introductory talk by one of the guides, and I would watch my audience carefully, because the dedicated Janeites would chuckle at the mere mention of Mr Collins's name. The more I discussed Jane Austen with the visitors, the more I saw how much she meant to so many people – and the more she came to mean to me.

By the time I left the Jane Austen Centre to pursue a career in the publishing industry, Jane Austen was firmly an all-time favourite author, second only perhaps to Charles Dickens. And she was – and remains – the only author whose life I know a lot about, whose biographies I read with fervour, who I think about in first name terms. Charles Dickens is still Dickens, but Jane Austen is *Jane*.

During that same year in Bath, I also started my BookTube channel. If you don't know about BookTube, it means You-Tube about books, and it is a glorious thing: a lively,

A Slow-burn Love Story

welcoming online community of readers. I have run my channel, Books and Things, for ten years now, and it's given me huge confidence, amazing book recommendations, and friends from all over the world – and it's also heightened my love for many of my favourite authors.

Back in 2018, I started the reading challenge Jane Austen July with my friend Marissa, who I'd met through BookTube. The idea was to have a month focused on Jane Austen and everything around her – reading the original novels, dipping our toes into her juvenilia and letters, tackling biographies, trying retellings and other authors from her time, watching screen adaptations. In this yearly celebration of Jane Austen, people from all over the world come together to read, discuss and make content about her books.

Over the past eight Jane Austen Julys, I've reread her books again and again. I've read, loved (and sometimes hated) retellings of her novels. I've watched countless adaptations and screen retellings. And I've discovered the joy of listening to her work on audiobook – reading aloud was a popular family entertainment in the eighteenth and nineteenth centuries, so most older novels were written to be read aloud. I've probably now listened to the Rosamund Pike audiobook of *Pride and Prejudice* even more times than I've read the physical book.

Reading Austen's novels socially and exchanging recommendations with others online has enriched my experience of her books. *Sense and Sensibility* was always my least favourite Austen – until, rereading it a couple of years ago, something finally clicked. Going in with different expectations helped shift my mindset. I stopped focusing on the slightly uneven pacing. I stopped thinking about how little we see of Edward Ferrars. I thought instead about the central themes: logic and emotion. I approached *Sense and Sensibility* as being as much a satire of the sentimental novel as *Northanger Abbey* is of the gothic novel, and suddenly I was reading it with new eyes.

Encounters with Jane Austen

One of the great joys of being a Jane Austen fan is that there are so many other Jane Austen fans. There are huge numbers of people talking and writing about her books, retelling them and adapting them to screen, talking about them on the internet and in everyday life. When you love Jane Austen, you become part of a huge Jane Austen metaverse: a network of readers and books interacting with and harking back to Jane Austen. I love reading Austen retellings and sequels, because each one demonstrates a unique reader's interpretation of the original work. And the way Jane Austen writes – her subtlety, the amount she leaves unsaid, how fully developed every side character is – gives so much space for retelling, for reinterpretation, for readers and writers to fill in the gaps.

There's no doubt that Jane Austen has had a huge influence on my own work as an author. I've learnt so much from her that I've tried to bring to my own writing: her use of wit and humour; the way she examines her themes; her deft methods of characterisation, her slight exaggerations and gentle caricatures, the complex way she builds her character arcs; her use of free indirect discourse, slipping into the voices of her characters.

My first novel, *The Secrets of Hartwood Hall*, is a gothic mystery, more directly influenced by the Brontës, who famously didn't think much of Jane Austen – or at least, Charlotte didn't; I have a suspicion Anne probably liked her more – but I've no doubt her influence still crept into my writing. And in my second novel, *The Trouble with Mrs Montgomery Hurst*, her impact is more obvious: the novel is set in 1841, at the start of the Victorian period, but the legacy of the Regency world is still very much felt by the characters. I wanted to capture a society on the cusp of something; the older generation grew up in the Regency period and have brought its values with them, but the younger characters are coming of age in a new era. I wanted to write a small-town story, a tale of gossip and community and

A Slow-burn Love Story

scandal, a novel about love and money and class – and who does all of that better than Jane Austen? There were many other literary influences on the novel – the Victorian writers Anthony Trollope and Elizabeth Gaskell especially – but I think and hope readers will find Jane Austen's fingerprints all over *The Trouble with Mrs Montgomery Hurst*.

But there are other lessons to be learnt from Austen, beyond her writing itself. She first finished a novel when she was in her late teens. She tried to get published aged twenty-one (*First Impressions*, later reworked into *Pride and Prejudice*, was rejected for publication in November 1797). Her novel *Northanger Abbey* (then entitled *Susan*) was sold to a publisher in spring 1803, when Jane Austen was twenty-seven years old – but it was never printed. Her first published novel, *Sense and Sensibility*, came out in 1811, around fifteen years after she'd first started work on it as an epistolary novel called *Elinor and Marianne*. Jane Austen was thirty-five years old, and she had been writing novels for the best part of two decades.

In some ways, we know so much about Jane Austen. We know her family tree, where she lived when, and her surviving letters offer a window into her personality. But in other ways, we don't know much about her. We don't even know what she looked like (the one portrait we have of her was said by her own family to be 'hideously unlike'). The 160 letters we have are only a small fraction of those she wrote over her lifetime, and when you read them, it's hard to tell what is real and what is wit. For example, much has been made of Jane Austen's early romance with Tom Lefroy, but when you read: 'At length the Day is come on which I am to flirt my last with Tom Lefroy ... My tears flow as I write, at the melancholy idea,' you do have to ask yourself: is she *joking*? Is she parodying sentimental novels in her letters, just as she does in her novels? How are we to find her true feelings beneath her wonderful humour?

But when I read about her slow, bumpy road to publication,

Encounters with Jane Austen

Jane Austen feels a lot less far away. This story of rejection and perseverance, reworking and editing and trying and trying again, will feel very familiar to many writers. It certainly feels familiar to me. (My 'first' novel, *The Secrets of Hartwood Hall*, was in fact the thirteenth I'd written.) There is a lot to learn from Jane Austen's writing, from her characterisation, her wit, her themes and her love stories – but there is also a lot to learn from Jane Austen herself, a person who loved writing and kept working on her books, determined to find an audience.

When I first read her novels as a teenager, I liked them – but over the past two decades, she has come to mean so much more to me. I've learnt from her as a writer and as a person, and the more I read and reread her books, the more comfort and interest they bring. Every time I read her novels, I discover something different. Each encounter with Jane Austen is new and rich and wonderful, and that's why I keep reading and rereading her books.

Katie Lumsden is an author, BookTuber and freelance editor based in London. She has written two historical novels, *The Secrets of Hartwood Hall* and *The Trouble with Mrs Montgomery Hurst*, the first of which was shortlisted for the Historical Writers' Association Debut Crown Award. Katie's YouTube channel, Books and Things, has over 33,000 subscribers, and each year she hosts two reading challenges focused on classic literature: Jane Austen July and Victober (Victorian October).

Words that blink

Esme Gutch

You're using words that kind of blink at me,
they sound just like the motion that I sense
they mean from how your hands, they fall between
our bodies like a bird's wing, or a fence.
And when eventually you turn away
it's like you tear the air behind by leaving.
I tremble like a glint of light that stays,
staying, can't still, itself, still interweaving.
Perhaps when all the swifts have flown the air,
have blown themselves like dandelion seeds
around the field and when the winds stir care
I wonder, might you try to reach to me?
I hear your voice, its echoing a song
I almost think I never knew at all.

Currently reading English at Hertford College, Oxford University. Founder of Hertford Poetry Society, poetry is an important part of both academic and wider aspects of her life. She is particularly interested in writing about relationships between people and the environment. She often composes poems in a notebook while walking on Ilkley Moor in Yorkshire, near her home.

Jane Austen and Shelley in the Garden

Janet Todd

Extracts from the novel[1].

Annie from Cambridge is sitting with her friend Fran in a Norfolk pub close to Fran's cottage.

Old age is an equalizer. It can, should they choose, be daisy-time together.

Jane Austen sits in a nook. 'I persevered', she remarks.

Fran stares towards the darkness. She knows exactly what Jane Austen thinks of her virtuosity, her magical tactile density. She also knows what she thinks of her Author's faux modesty: those little pieces of ivory she claimed to be writing on with little effect. Really!

'Some readers say my books repeat themselves', continues Jane Austen, 'pretty girl catches eligible man: common romances. Not so. Only a jealous person understands real love, it's always one-sided. Fanny Price, my Mansfield heroine with the undiverted heart.'

---

1 *Jane Austen and Shelley in the Garden: A Novel with Pictures.* Fentum Press, 2021. A (light) meditation on age, loneliness, and hope which concerns three women from the post-war generation; one of them (Fran) has let herself be haunted by Jane Austen.
The women are approaching retirement: they feel they have, for the first time in their lives, a choice in their manner of living. They unite in a quest for the idealist poet Percy Bysshe Shelley. On their travels together they discuss motherhood, death, feminism, the resurgence of childhood memories in old age, as well as the tensions between generations.

Jane Austen and Shelley in the Garden

'You betrayed her: you said she'd have taken another man.'

'I am a realist. I deal in probabilities.'

'*Pride and Prejudice*: the girl who gets it all?'

'Things exactly as they are', murmurs Jane Austen dreamily from her nook contemplating the technicolour twentieth century. A crimson horse and blue guitar.

She pulls herself back to her time. 'One must earn pewter.'

'You created weak Fanny Price to atone for Lizzie Bennet's ludicrous vivid luck – no virtue in being healthy…'

Fran washes her hands perfunctorily in the cloakroom. The air dryer isn't working, so she rubs them on her stiff hemp jacket. She returns to find Annie by the door, only just restraining impatience.

'A mind lively and at ease, can do with seeing nothing, and can see nothing that does not answer,' whispers Jane Austen in Fran's ear. She channels Emma, a character for whom she has a very soft spot.

Irritated, Fran turns back. 'Emma never sees 'nothing'. What she sees is half imaginary, the rest just theatre.'

Jane Austen smirks. Author and character are imaginists: they see nothing to see everything.

She swishes out the door, leaving only the faintest whiff of that wicked narrative voice.

…

*

Fran sits on her small double bed in her cottage. She contemplates Jane Austen sidling into the room.

'A little perambulating round Southern England but otherwise such stability! How'd you have coped with rootlessness, nomadism without tent and tribe?' (Can one envy a ghost?) 'You needed midwives in life and work. You'd have been a lady writing upstairs on her little writing table without the handy brothers. Waiting on a curate or pompous college fellow to remove the shame of spinsterhood.'

'Got that off your chest?' sniggers Jane Austen. 'You are so residually Victorian: my sister and I never thought of women as spinsters, surplus or odd. We were ladies – I, in addition, was an Author.'

'It's a point of view.'

Why do a Mary Wollstonecraft: splattered on her path through life by mud from contemptuous boots and hooves? Being what? A poor teacher, companion, governess, hack writer, exhibitionist of women's rights. Surely better loll in a warm family carriage, not your own – or your own woman perhaps – but always a lady?

'I had no command of the carriage,' protests Jane Austen. 'It was not yet the Age of Woman. You can't anticipate history, though you can adjust it, as your age is doing. I kept it at my back.'

Fran's rebuked. She knows as well as Jane Austen the humiliating lack of control one has over one's life and culture. Does one have a duty to be mutinous?

Despite her tartness, thinks Fran, Jane Austen makes the world a little less cold than it might otherwise be, even in a drafty attic. The most important thing is resilience, elasticity of mind.

'And virtue,' says Jane Austen from the door.

Fran ignores her.

...

*

'I see myself caught in a reliquary,' mutters Jane Austen, 'surrounded by polished carving.'

'Which part of you is in the casket?' asks Fran. 'A bit of bone, a finger, a tooth?'

Jane Austen and Shelley in the Garden

'Tongue, hand. It's a posthumous feeling: constricted as I am now by peacock embellishments. Still, I know life and posterity are mere anterooms.'

A lapsed Baptist, Fran keeps thoughts to herself. Jane Austen is a Believer. Though nowadays the Church of England barely counts, it's still some distance from secular relativism. Did Jane Austen ever doubt?

Once as a child Fran watched faith die, right before her eyes. The minister had a house, a car and a (small) flock from the chapel, all depending on belief in Pentecostal flame. In late middle age, how would he learn another trade? He went on preaching.

Had it really happened in so counter damascene a way? Baptists love a drama: factor that in.

Later, the minister was accused of 'backsliding'. Fran imagined him gliding on his rump down the slippery slope towards the lake of infidel perdition, arms folded.

She doesn't often mention her lax sectarian past to Jane Austen. Despite a generous gesture towards evangelicals in a letter, the Author never cared for Nonconformists. At heart she was a traditionalist, a thoughtful, discerning, critical traditionalist.

Are no probabilities to be accepted, merely because they are not certainties?

'Would I have inspired Austenolatry had I let Sir Thomas Bertram drone on about slavery in *Mansfield Park*?'

If he'd done so, he might have revealed what is probable, thought Fran, that he was an ameliorist – like her reverend father. An unacceptable position now we see the delicate negotiations of the past in the most lurid light. Jane Austen ignored Fran's thoughts on slavery – or she'd have had to mount her high horse.

Fran surveys herself in the mottled mirror on the inside of

Encounters with Jane Austen

the wardrobe door. 'Who are you?' she says.

The mirror image smirks.

Though eccentric, the action improves on her habit of staring at Cassandra's crude sketch so fixedly that the aslant eyes swivel to catch hers. That really is naughty.

She never copies that poker-rigid back so thrillingly watercoloured by her sister. Probably done at the seaside but you can never be sure. The hidden eyes see nothing.

'I was not,' murmurs Jane Austen, 'taken unawares when my dear sister sketched my likeness. I knew exactly what I was presenting: Cassandra and I had excellent posture.'

What are men to rocks and mountains? says Lizzie Bennet, heading for the barren Lake District.

She's waylaid by the romantic plot, some strategy – and that luck. But she might have gone.

Do you go to a place or does the place come to you?

Jane Austen's busy climbing into the wardrobe ignoring its mirrored door.

There are moments when Fran is defiantly angry with the Author and her free indirect manner. Such an easy way to watch others deceive themselves. For now, she simply feels deflated by this quick removal.

Until she thinks: Jane Austen, the Witch in the Wardrobe.

...

*

Fran meets Annie's friends, scholars of the Romantic poet, Shelley. Fran will travel with them to Venice,

Some of the poet Shelley's expenses:
  A Superfine Olive Coat Gilt Buttons 4 8 0
  A Pair Rich Silk Knitt Pantaloons 3 8 0
  Two Stripd Marcela Waistcoats Double Breastd 2 0 0.

Jane Austen and Shelley in the Garden

Pair Patent Silk Braces 0 8 0

A Superfine Blue Coat Velvett Collr & Gilt Buttns 4 12 0

Jane Austen gulps. She thinks of those bonnet trimmings and collar turnings, the tedious mending of petticoats and socks. 'I am a gentleman's daughter' is the proud boast of all her heroines – except perhaps poor Fanny Price – yet it can't equal this. The 'large fortune' you know.

Fran's impressed. 'Did he ever pay for these items?'

She knows the answer: not something that concerns a negligent aristocrat.

In my 'Beautiful Cassandra', adds Jane Austen, even as a child I was aware of such carelessness. Eating six ices from a pastry cook without paying. What a noble fantasy.

...

*

What, pray, is the difference in memory between seeing a place and reading of it, looking directly or through an image?

In the Middle Ages one might receive indulgence for sins by doing pilgrimage to a decent copy of a shrine.

Lord Byron sees the ordinary within the extraordinary. Venice is perhaps his most creative time: excess writing, excess sex. He wrote to his publisher John Murray:

"There's a whore on my right

For I rhyme best at night."

'"My" John Murray,' adds Jane Austen, 'was a rogue, he would have drooled over such salacious letters.'

'Murray was generous to you,' mutters Fran, 'you and your brother miscalculated. You thought your copyright more valuable than it was.'

Jane Austen is remembering her amazing future worth. In the long run...

In the long run we are all dead.

Encounters with Jane Austen

'My sea,' remarks Jane Austen, 'is not lonely. My naval heroes force enemy ships to surrender, they wrest riches from storms. Its bluster gives bloom to my girls – dear Fanny Price on Portsmouth ramparts, perfect Anne Elliot on the Cobb at Lyme. Venice is built on a swamp: at best one might say it fronts a flat lagoon. 'Lagoon' is a lonely word.

'Don't stay if you feel like that,' retorts Fran.

No opening for pertness and sardonic quips. (People get tetchy when travelling.) 'I didn't tell you to come.'

'Italy with its pines and vices, Mrs Radcliffe's gothic town? Why would I not? '

How quick come the reasons for approving what we like, smiles Fran.

The Author purses her lips. One cannot creep upon a journey.

...

*

At the end of the novel Fran and Annie plan to move together into a new house.

Fran's in Norfolk preparing the cottage for sale, knowing it will take time to shift. She's moving any cuteness from living spaces; the pink China pig and Johnnie's blue owl go from the fireplace.

She begins on deep cleaning. She scrubs the dirtiest parts of the kitchen floor, then attacks the smudged, fat-stained stove. From time to time she looks through the little window to see if the regular blackbird has come. It hasn't, so she listens instead to the cooing and plonking of pigeons. The stove is now brighter but still smudged; it shows up the grubbiness of counter tops and wooden cabinet doors.

Is Fran having an old-age crisis? She regards her gardening hands. Thin paper skin stretching like poor soil over rocky veins.

Jane Austen and Shelley in the Garden

Jane Austen doesn't see housework as 'work'. 'Never mistake my life for yours,' snaps the Author. 'We women always had servants, a goodly number, even at our poorest. You have transport and can go where you wish, but I, with only a donkey cart, was always served. I was never on my knees in a garden or on a kitchen floor.'

Fran has cleaned the teak banana bench on which the hawk had shat, bought new bushes to look pretty by spring, rewilded a sunny verge with native seeds, rooting out modern hybrids that might repel the sophisticated second-home buyer. Every plant in the garden must be hardy or easily replaceable. All will be tidy. The wild strawberries are gone.

Jane Austen is again muttering about fruit, set off by the mention of strawberries. Mrs Jennings stuffing on mulberries, Mrs Norris's apricot no tastier than Dr Grant's potato, General Tilney boasting of pineapples, Mrs Elton gorging on Donwell's gourmet strawberries.

'Why this displacing of vulgarity onto fruit?' smiles Fran. 'You never saw Bosch's fleshly nudes devouring gargantuan strawberries.'

'Shakespeare called them wholesome berries. I am always with the Bard. Did you know your 'amiable' Anne Boleyn had a strawberry birthmark proving her a witch and St Hildegard of Bingen rejected fruit that creeps with snakes and toads along the ground?'

Fran hums now as she pulls up nettles and dead plants, murmuring, 'Sweet place, all nature has a feeling, landscape listens.'

Despite her poetizing their earthy pull, she knows the cottage and garden have demanded too much maintenance: her trees are overbearing, her flowers too needy. The trip to Venice had dark moments but, on the whole, even with a tendency to overcloud in memory, it had been more than usually bright.

Encounters with Jane Austen

She sees Jane Austen strolling by the bare apple tree quoting lines from Cowper's 'Sofa':

"The sloping land recedes into the clouds.

Displaying on its varied side the grace

Of hedgerow beauties numberless."

It's not the season, thinks Fran, but no matter. Words and things don't necessarily coalesce. She ambles over to meet her Author.

'You haven't always made my life better here,' she says, 'with your caution, civility and repression, your maddening romantic endings.'

'As ever, you misinterpret me,' replies Jane Austen serenely. 'You were never a good close reader. Besides, we have all a better guide in ourselves, if we would attend to it, than any other person can be.'

Fran walks swiftly back into the warm house mumbling what not even she can hear.

Later she packs up her editions of the sacred works in their different formats: reprinted paperbacks in new covers with bonneted girls looking through saucy modern eyes; annotated hardbacks with Hugh Thomson illustrations; comic versions of *Pride and Prejudice*.

'You'll look well in our new garden, by the hollyhocks. You can serve expensive teas on rosy plates when the sky's blue. Celebrity has responsibilities.'

'I am no enthusiast of hollyhocks,' replies Jane Austen, 'a Victorian taste. I will need pinks, sweet Williams, columbines, cornflowers, Cowper's ivory-pure syringa, his laburnum rich in streaming gold. Fruits and flowers,' she murmurs again, 'flowers and fruits.'

Fran waits for her to continue. Surely, she must have more

Jane Austen and Shelley in the Garden

to say to ladies planning to live together.

'It's best,' remarks Jane Austen after a pause, 'to keep ailments private. Old age, frailty, decline and death: it is no use to lament. As I remarked shortly before dying, I never heard that even Mary Queen of Scots' lamentation did her any good, so could not expect benefit from mine. We are all sorry, and now that subject is exhausted.'

The Author flexes her fingers inside an expensive pair of red leather gloves. As a child she went gloveless, but maturity brings covering of parts.

Janet Todd began investigating early women writers in the early 1970s in the US, beginning with the then little known Aphra Behn and Mary Wollstonecraft. In recent years she has worked much on Jane Austen, her most recent book being *Living with Jane Austen* which came out from CUP in 2025 along with a new edition of the fiction in 8 volumes. Janet is a former President of Lucy Cavendish College, Cambridge.

Untitled

Karenjit Sandhu

she left the house
shut the door behind
                      /////
                      |||

detestable /
       vexed
                /

   affronted
/
as the wildberries scraped
    her heels,
she felt the heave of loss
                  not letting her head
                  go there _____
   this one last time
back behind she went
   |||
to the nidgetty! too nidgetty to please!
they said
                      /////

Untitled

Karenjit Sandhu's publications include *gestalt* and *young girls!* (The 87 Press), *Poetic Fragments from the Irritating Archive* (Guillemot Press) and *Baby 19* (Intergraphia Books). Her work also appears in *Judith: Women Making Visual Poetry* and *The Blue Notebook: Journal for Artists' Books*. She is a member of the British Art Network and Lecturer in Art at the Reading School of Art.

*"I wish,
as well as everybody else,
to be perfectly happy;
but, like everybody else,
it must be in my own way."*

– Sense and Sensibility

She wanted to compose her own feelings and to make
herself agreeable to all.

The maquette made at one-third scale of statue of Jane Austen
Photo: Steve Russell Studios

Sculpting Jane

Interview with sculptor Martin Jennings

Martin Jennings has made a new bronze sculpture of Jane Austen for Winchester Cathedral.

How did you become a sculptor?

Well, I come from an artistic family. My mother was a painter. My father was an aspirant painter who became a headmaster. And we were always brought up looking at paintings and drawings and to admire the great writers and artists above all others. I did a degree in English literature and that was followed by a year at art school and an apprenticeship to a craftsman. Initially, I moved into the world of lettering, carving inscriptions in stone and slate and using other materials to make lettering for architectural and monumental purposes. And then, slowly and steadily, I progressed into figurative sculpture and that's where I persist though I do carve the odd inscription to go with my sculptures.

Can you tell me about some of your commissions? Any favourites?

It's hard to consider any of them my favorites; each time I go back to look at them, I think how I wish I could improve them. Over the last 25 years of my work, I've tended to make sculptures of authors. One seems to have led to another. There's been John Betjeman, Philip Larkin, George Orwell, John Keats, and now Jane Austen. And interspersed with that, there've been public statues of famous medics like Archibald McIndoe, Mary Seacole and the odd politician. One I am pleased with is the statue of the Women of Steel in Sheffield – the women who worked in the steel industries in the Second and First World Wars. It's been varied work, but it's always been interesting.

How did you come to be commissioned to make the Jane Austen sculpture?

I was approached by the Interim Dean Roland Riem, about seven or eight years ago. He had seen my previous sculptures of authors and thought I'd be the right person to make one of Jane Austen. The site eventually chosen, the Inner Close at Winchester Cathedral is where she'll stand.

How did you decide on the pose and the size?

We went through various iterations of it for different sites within the Inner Close. Initially the aspiration was that it should be a large figure in an open site in front of the deanery. When we changed the site to a smaller, more enclosed lawn within the Close, that required a slightly smaller piece. So it's only about six foot high, about 1.1 times life size, which is a scale that is appropriate for the more domestic space it occupies.

Is that near to the gravestone inside Winchester Cathedral?

That's inside Winchester Cathedral, whereas my sculpture is outside. But she will be looking towards the cathedral, which is a building that her sister recorded her as greatly admiring. So there will be a direct association. It's always important to think when you make a figurative sculpture what it's looking at.

Please tell me about the process of making the statue. Can you describe the various stages?

I made a maquette, a scale model, and it went through two or three quite significant changes. I proposed one version which was not generally favoured; it was a bit too grandiose for the site. It was not only Jane Austen, but it involved a kind of screen behind her with the branches of a tree running across it. What we now have is a simpler version, a representation

Sculpting Jane

Rear view: The maquette made at one-third scale of statue of Jane Austen. Photo: Steve Russell Studios

of Austen rising from her tiny little writing desk at Chawton. The conceit is that she's at home, she's writing, there's one of her notebooks, an inkwell and a quill on the table. Somebody has come to the door and she's rising to meet this person and semi-hiding her work behind her. So I wanted to make a point about the difficulty of pursuing your profession as a woman at the time with the endless interrruptions. It also gave the opportunity for a degree of movement in the sculpture. I think there's something to be gained when you make a figurative sculpture in posing the figure in a movement that is about to be resolved but hasn't been yet. And because when you look at that sort of thing, it induces a very slight degree of tension that generates an emotional connection with a piece of work.

It's a sort of dramatic moment caught in time?

I hope so. It's a representation of her indoors placed out of doors, and anyone who's been to Chawton will recognize that little table she wrote at, which is so surprising. There's a point to be made about how such great works came from such little beginnings.

Is the statue being cast at a foundry in the UK?

Yes, it's being cast in Gloucestershire by Pangolin Editions foundry, which I've been with for the whole of my sculpting career. They're now the biggest in the West and I think the best in the world. Once I finished the clay version of the sculpture, a six-part mold was taken of it. From that mold you can create a positive impression in a thin layer of wax. The wax is then encased in a heatproof grog. So you end up with a large boulder-like form of grogged plaster with this piece of wax inside it. Bearing in mind there are six pieces of wax to make up the whole of this six-foot-high figure. That boulder-like shape is put into a kiln and the wax is melted out. Into the gap left by the wax you pour molten bronze and then begins a long process of filing and welding the metals to recreate exactly what I modeled in clay.

Sculpting Jane

So essentially is it hollow in the middle?

Yes, it would be extremely heavy if it wasn't. The figure might look solid but it's actually only about a quarter of an inch thick all round.

What colour has been chosen for the finish?

This is likely to be a dark green.

Who made the choice and why?

I made the choice. And the cathedral have so far agreed to that and I think they're happy with the idea. Betjeman and Larkin, some of my previous sculptures, have both been dark green metal. It has a less ponderous, more culturally appropriate feel to it. It's friendlier perhaps than the dark browns that you see on so many sculptures and can seem quite beautiful. This sculpture will sit on a lawn on a very low plinth. The green patina emphasizes the connection with nature around it.

How was the money raised for the statue?

It took a while to raise the money and that was all done by Roland Riem and the cathedral mainly from private donors.

Did it take around five years?

Yes, I would say about five years. It's very difficult to raise money for a public figurative sculpture at the moment, not least because there's a considerable degree of uncertainty, even embarrassment about public statues. People don't quite know what to do with them these days. And it all started with the sculpture of the slave trader Colston being dumped in the harbour in Bristol. But it set off a long conversation about what the function and purpose of these things is in public spaces. I would argue that when they're good works of art and they represent people who deserve them, they can be very pleasing and laudable objects.

Encounters with Jane Austen

Do you think it's important to celebrate women of achievement? To redress the lack of statues of women of achievement.

Absolutely, yes. Something like 15% of statues are of women and I think half of those are of Queen Victoria.

If you remove the royals and the mythical figures of women I think it's only 3% of public statues are representative of women of achievement.

Yes, there's a balance to be redressed and I hope to play my part in that with statues of people like Mary Seacole, Jane Austen and the Women of Steel.

Why do you think Jane Austen is so popular today?

I think she's always been popular, hasn't she? To different generations. I think it's the exactness of her perception of social interaction. It's her irony and her wit. Such beautifully drawn characters. It's the clear hierarchy between the dominant figures in her dramas and the lower tier of figures who are never allowed to become mere cutouts. They all have their part to play. It's the close observation of human foibles. It's all delivered in prose of such refined quality. I don't know what more one can say. I mean I love her novels and always have.

She asks the question how to live a moral life and she shows characters failing and making mistakes and getting things wrong, which is very human.

She never allows the characters who commit the most harm not to come across as human despite their faults. And sometimes it's hilarious and sometimes it's pretty alarming when you look at the way that someone like Wickham behaves in *Pride and Prejudice* or Lady Catherine de Bourgh, whose spite is acutely seen. There is absolutely a moral vision running through it, even though you couldn't describe her, particularly, as a Christian author. She happened to be a Christian; we're placing her in front of the cathedral. But the Christian religion is not at the forefront of Austen's novels even though they are shot through with her moral vision.

What will be the benefit to Winchester of having a statue there at the cathedral?

I hope that people will come to see it and that it will further cement the relationship between Austen and the cathedral city of her county. She admired the cathedral but she didn't live in Winchester. She came there in the last weeks of her life and died there only a couple of streets away from the cathedral. She lived in Hampshire for the majority of her life apart from her time in Bath. So I think it will reaffirm her connection with the county and with Winchester. It will bring people in to see the cathedral and to see the city who might not otherwise have visited because now they will have a clearer association between them and Jane Austen.

It's a visual representation of her, and it's not far from Chawton so you could do both the cathedral and her house in the same day?

Absolutely. That is if people like the statue as a representation of her! People have very strong feelings about how she should be represented. I've been surprised at the fervour with which people care about this. I haven't met it with any of the other authors I've represented.

Interesting, because there's only one sketch of her. Isn't there one small drawing by her sister Cassandra?

Yes. Or rather, there's a view of her from behind by Cassandra as well, but you can't really tell from that what she looked like. Jane Austen's niece said that Cassandra's portrait was not a good likeness. Looking at it, it's probably a 10 to 15 minute sketch. And Cassandra was a hesitant artist. So it is quite light evidence as to what Jane Austen looked like. The stronger evidence is in the written record, that she had a very slim figure; the drawing by Cassandra suggests that she was more homely. And as far as we can tell that is not the case. There is a pelisse, which is a kind

Encounters with Jane Austen

of dressing gown, still in existence, that she had made for her, which shows her figure to be extremely slight.

It was tried on by various people in recent years and they could only get it to fit a very slim teenage girl. It was made for Austen when she was in her late thirties. So there's that. And then the written record suggests that she had quite a long nose, small mouth, large eyes. And I've included those. But it's largely a form of speculation and I hope I haven't made it too unlike what people imagined she looked like. From Cassandra's drawing, further enhanced in the Victorian era and now represented on our bank notes, you wouldn't expect her to be as slender as the other evidence proves.

Have you been asked to try and capture the spirit of the person? How can you do that?

You do your best, you do your reading, you know your character. You infer your character from the reading. So for example, when I was making the John Betjeman statue, I read all of his poetry more than once. From that you get the tenour of the person you are dealing with. So biography is useful up to a point. But in fact the works tell you who someone was, and you try to transfer that into the sculpture. It's a subjective thing. I mean it's my interpretation, it's one interpretation of Austen and it won't please everybody, but I hope it'll be acceptable to enough people. People do hold her close to their hearts. Her enthusiastic supporters talk of her as if she was their close friend and they will have a strong notion of who that person is. This is my interpretation and I hope I've got something of her in there.

She was more of an observer? Always observing people.

She was, but what I have mostly hoped to convey in the sculpture is her authority as a writer. She was physically slight but the image of strength.

Sculpting Jane

Martin Jennings has been making public sculpture in Britain for many years. His representations of great writers and poets are particularly well-known: John Betjeman at St Pancras Station, Philip Larkin in Hull, Charles Dickens in Portsmouth and George Orwell outside BBC Broadcasting House.

Celebrated figures from the medical profession have also featured prominently, with John Radcliffe in Oxford, Archibald McIndoe in East Grinstead and Mary Seacole outside St Thomas' Hospital in London. His sculpture of prime minister Stanley Baldwin stands in Bewdley, Worcestershire, and a seated figure of actor Ronnie Barker in Aylesbury.

His sculptures are cast in bronze with accompanying text carved in stone or slate around them. The Women of Steel in Sheffield and George Orwell at the BBC each received the national PMSA Marsh Award for Excellence in Public Sculpture in 2017 and 2018

Witch-Wife

Edna St. Vincent Millay

She is neither pink nor pale,
And she never will be all mine;
She learned her hands in a fairy-tale,
And her mouth on a valentine.

She has more hair than she needs;
In the sun 'tis a woe to me!
And her voice is a string of coloured beads,
Or steps leading into the sea.

She loves me all that she can
And her ways to my ways resign;
But she was not made for any man,
And she never will be all mine.

Witch-Wife

Edna St. Vincent Millay (1892-1950) was a renowned American poet and playwright. She also became well-known as a feminist writer while living in the bohemian hotspot of Greenwich Village. Gaining in popularity, during her twenties, Millay won the 1923 Pulitzer Prize for Poetry for her fourth book, *Ballad of the Harp-Weaver* becoming the first woman to win the award. In 1943, Millay was also awarded the Frost Medal for her lifetime contribution to American poetry. She also wrote under the pseudonym Nancy Boyd.

She coined the popular phrase, "My candle burns at both ends," and the literary critic Edmund Wilson, an admirer, said of her "one of the only poets writing in English in our time who has attained to anything like the stature of great literary figures."

She married Dutch businessman Eugen Boissevain who supported her career. The couple purchased a 700-acre farm in Austerlitz, New York, known as Steepletop. Millay died there in 1950, and is buried in the grounds.

The rise of feminist literary criticism in the 1960s and 1970s revived an interest in Millay's work.

Jane Austen and the Gothic Novel

Ellen Cheshire

It is a truth universally acknowledged that a reader seeking a tale of terror and romance would have to wait until the 1760s for the Gothic novel to be 'invented'. Horace Walpole's *The Castle of Otranto* (1764) is widely considered the starting point of the genre. Although somewhat shorter than many later additions, it introduced many essential tropes: haunted castles, mysterious abbeys, secret passages, ghosts, curses, noble heroes, tormented villains, skeletons, gruesome events and innocent young women under threat.

The heroines of these dark romantic tales frequently sought out danger, foolishly opening the door behind which a strange noise lurks or placing themselves deliberately in peril. Suggesting a hidden craving for excitement – a boldness that drives them to confront the unknown, even as they fear it. At the same time, they are portrayed as sentimental and emotionally delicate, their vulnerability leaving them in need of rescue. Their saviours are typically poor but noble young men: earnest and virtuous. Yet not all men in these stories are so honourable. They were also populated by charming, roguish villains: educated, eloquent and morally corrupt, who seduce or deceive for their own ends. And if not endangered by these attractive men, the young women were often at the mercy of tyrannical fathers or guardians who imprison or coerce them, intensifying the atmosphere of entrapment. Together, these figures create the dramatic tensions that define the genre, with the heroine caught between desire, danger, and the hope of deliverance.

Jane Austen and the Gothic Novel

Jane Austen, well acquainted with these conventions, both parodied and engaged with them across her novels – most notably in *Northanger Abbey* – using their contradictions to explore the complexities of her own characters.

Born in 1775, Jane Austen was a voracious reader from a young age, exploring her father's extensive library of novels, poetry and history. Her Juvenilia, written between the ages of 11 and 18, brim with sharp humour and irreverence, critiquing social and literary norms – including the Gothic literature that had become enormously popular by the 1780s and 1790s. Advances in print technology made books more affordable and the rise of circulating libraries made them accessible to a wider public. At its peak, around 25 Gothic novels were published each year – around 35 per cent of all fiction output.[1] Capitalising further on this trend, publishers like the Minerva Press rapidly churned out thousands of tales of terror and romance, often cheaply made and poorly edited, but accessible to the growing mass market. They fascinated readers with themes the Enlightenment sought to dismiss: irrationality, emotion, the supernatural, and mystery.

Ann Radcliffe (1764-1823) was a central figure in establishing Gothic literary traditions and highly influential on its development. Her most famous works included *The Romance of the Forest* (1791), *The Mysteries of Udolpho* (1794) and *The Italian* (1797). She famously favoured 'terror' over 'horror', emphasising psychological suspense and the sublime – those overwhelming feelings of awe and fear inspired by vast, mysterious landscapes or intense emotional experiences – rather than graphic or grotesque imagery. One of her signature techniques was the use of the 'explained supernatural', where seemingly ghostly or uncanny events were ultimately revealed to have rational causes. This created a delicate tension between the

---

1 Frayling, Christopher. 'We Live in Gothic times...' in *The Gothic Reader: A Critical Anthology* (p12), edited by Martin Myrone. Tate Publishing. 2006.

real and the imaginary, suggesting that fear often arises from the unknown and that understanding dispels terror. Deeply familiar with Radcliffe's work, Austen engages with these established genre traditions in *Northanger Abbey* (1818) with characteristic wit, both paying homage to its thrilling early forms and critiquing the reassuring predictability it later acquired. Her engagement with Gothic conventions also surfaces in allusions and character types throughout her other novels.

Jane Austen's *Northanger Abbey*, though published posthumously in December 1817, was thought to have been begun and extensively worked on around 1798–99[2], at the height of the genre's craze. Its heroine, Catherine Morland, is obsessed with popular tales of horror and passion. When she stays at Northanger Abbey as a guest of the Tilneys, her imagination runs wild, leading her to suspect all manner of melodramatic horrors where none exist. The novel stands as a witty parody of the Gothic novel.

In 1816, Austen wrote a preface to the novel, explaining that she had originally intended to publish it in 1803 and apologising for what might now appear "comparatively obsolete." Janet Todd[3], in *Living with Jane Austen*, reflects on this phrase, wondering whether Austen was referring to the mockery of the Gothic or the attention to women's fashions – both of which had changed dramatically in the intervening years. Austen would have appeared ahead of the curve had *Northanger Abbey* been published in 1803 as she had originally intended, but by 1817 Eaton Stannard Barrett's *The Heroine; or, Adventures of a Fair Romance Reader* (1813) had already taken aim at the overwrought tropes of the genre. The novel chronicles the misadventures of Cherry Wilkinson, a young woman so overwhelmed by her obsession with Gothic romances that

---

2 Butler, Marilyn. *Jane Austen and the War of Ideas* (p. 169), Clarendon Press (Oxford University Press). 1975.
3 Todd, Janet. *Living with Jane Austen* (p 87). Cambridge University Press. 2025.

Jane Austen and the Gothic Novel

she tries to live out the role of a heroine herself, fabricating scandals, fainting at inconvenient times and misinterpreting innocent people as dangerous villains. Like Catherine Morland, Cherry is both a victim of her imagination and a comic figure of excess, but while Austen's treatment of Catherine is gentle and affectionate, Barrett's satire is more biting and sustained. His novel skewers not only the genre's conventions but also the perceived moral dangers of unrestrained female reading.

Barrett's novel was a commercial success and won praise from Austen herself. In a letter to her sister Cassandra dated 2nd–3rd March 1814, she wrote that she had "torn through the 3d vol. of the *Heroine*, & do not think it falls off. – It is a delightful burlesque, particularly on the Radcliffe style."[4] This endorsement underscores how Austen not only shared Barrett's awareness of Gothic excess but admired his execution of it.

Although Austen had continued revising *Northanger Abbey* on and off over the intervening decades until her death in July 1817, the novel was not published until December of that year, when her brother Henry arranged for its posthumous release alongside *Persuasion*. Just weeks later, in January 1818, Mary Shelley's *Frankenstein* appeared anonymously in London. The timing is notable: Austen's novel satirises the Gothic conventions popularised by writers like Ann Radcliffe, while Shelley's work signals the emergence of a darker, more philosophical strain of the tradition. In this way, *Northanger Abbey* captures a transitional moment, looking back with irony at late-18th-century sentimental terrors even as the Gothic evolved toward the existential and psychological depths explored in 19th-century contributions to the genre.

As Claire Harman notes in *Jane's Fame*[5], Austen's greatness

---
4 Austen, Jane in a letter to her sister Cassandra, 2nd-3rd March 1814, as quoted on Jane Austen's House website. https://janeaustens.house/object/the-mysteries-of-udolpho/ [last accessed 26/6/25]
5 Harman, Claire. *Jane's Fame: How Jane Austen Conquered the World* (p. 33). Cannongate. 2009

Encounters with Jane Austen

as a writer stemmed in part from her voracious and eclectic reading habits, guided by pleasure and shaped by an astute, consumer-like understanding of the genres she most enjoyed. This deep familiarity informs *Northanger Abbey*, where Austen playfully exposes the excesses of the genre and the uncritical enthusiasm of those who devour its pages. At the same time, she offers insight into the literary culture of her era, capturing both the genre's mass appeal and the emergence of a more self-aware reading public.

One of the novel's most striking meta-fictional moments comes when Catherine Morland's friend Isabella Thorpe recommends a list of Gothic titles – works that became known, thanks to Austen's endorsement, as the 'Northanger Horrid Novels':

1. *The Castle of Wolfenbach* by Eliza Parsons (1793)
2. *Clermont* by Regina Maria Roche (1798)
3. *The Mysterious Warning* by Eliza Parsons (1796)
4. *The Necromancer* by Karl Friedrich Kahlert (1794; English translation 1795)
5. *The Midnight Bell* by Francis Lathom (1798)
6. *The Orphan of the Rhine* by Eleanor Sleath (1798)
7. *Horrid Mysteries* by the Marquis de Grosse (original German publication 1796; English translation 1797)

These are not fictitious inventions, as was once believed, but real novels that circulated widely in the 1790s and early 1800s. Renewed interest in early Gothic fiction has led to their rediscovery, confirming their popularity during Austen's lifetime. Their former obscurity now underscores Austen's intimate knowledge of contemporary fiction and the breadth of her literary satire.

The line spoken by Isabella Thorpe to Catherine Morland, "But are they all horrid? Are you sure they are all horrid?"[6] – functions as a clever in-joke. It is at once affectionate teasing

---
6 Austen, Jane. Chapter 6. *Northanger Abbey*.

Jane Austen and the Gothic Novel

and a subtle commentary on shifting literary hierarchies, revealing Austen's keen awareness of the divide between refined literary taste and mass-market sensationalism published by Minerva et al.

But it is the more established and revered Ann Radcliffe with whom Austen most directly engages. "While I have *Udolpho* to read," declares Catherine, "I feel as if nobody could make me miserable."[7] This line captures both the emotional intensity and escapist pull of Radcliffe's fiction. *The Mysteries of Udolpho* is not only the most frequently mentioned novel in *Northanger Abbey*, but also the one that most profoundly shapes Catherine's imagination. Austen cleverly plays with Radcliffe's hallmark of the 'explained supernatural,' contrasting Catherine's heightened, Gothic expectations – conjured by her voracious reading of *Udolpho* – with the mundane realities she encounters at Northanger Abbey. In doing so, Austen transforms Radcliffe's influence into a central mechanism for both humour and character development.

There is a distinctly affectionate tone in *Northanger Abbey*'s treatment of these novels and their readers. Austen's narrator – unseen yet unmistakably present – does not merely dismiss the so-called "horrid" books; rather, she gently satirises how young readers like Catherine and Isabella adopt them as an emotional shorthand, a shared language rich with notions of danger, excitement and youthful rebellion. Wandering the genteel streets of Bath, attending afternoon teas and dances, the girls revel in their nocturnal reading, breathlessly recounting the tales' excesses and excitements as if they were real-life events. Their enthusiasm mirrors the way modern teenagers might obsess over teen horror films or dark fantasy TV series, gripped by their intensity and united by shared passion. In this way, these thrilling stories become more than just entertainment; they serve as a means of constructing

---

7 Ibid.

identity, escaping the mundane and testing the limits of the known world.

Catherine's deep immersion in thrilling tales, in turn, sets the stage for the comically misguided misunderstandings that are the driving force of the novel. A vivid example occurs when Catherine begins to suspect General Tilney of having murdered or imprisoned his wife, her thoughts shaped entirely by the dark intrigues of the Gothic novels she devours: "Could it be possible? Could Henry's father – ? And yet why not? There were instances of wives being kept in confinement for life by their husbands."[8]

This moment reveals how Catherine's symbolic engagement with Gothic fiction clouds her judgement, as she reads sinister intent into the ordinary. Austen gently mocks this leap of imagination while maintaining sympathy for Catherine, whose ideas are drawn directly from her favourite books. The narrator's tone here is ironic but warm, reminding the reader that Catherine's confusion is both a satire of genre conventions and a commentary on the limitations of female experience and education, which leave young women to interpret the world through fiction.

Throughout, the narrator's intimate and confidential tone creates the effect of a personal dialogue, as if Austen herself were taking the reader aside with a knowing smile. Rather than dismissing her heroine's wild imaginings, Austen shows how stories – however outlandish – can shape hopes, fears and the way we make sense of the world. Beneath the amusement there's a quiet recognition of how little guidance society offers young women, and how easily imagination rushes in to fill the gaps.

Amid the novel's playful dialogue with Gothic conventions, the male characters embody contrasting responses to both Catherine's imagination and the social realities she navigates. Henry Tilney stands out as a quietly radical figure: intelligent,

---

8 Austen, Jane. Chapter 23. *Northanger Abbey*.

Jane Austen and the Gothic Novel

witty and emotionally perceptive. One who understands the limits and possibilities of Gothic fantasy. Unlike his domineering father, General Tilney, whose cold authoritarianism evokes the Gothic trope of the tyrannical patriarch, or his flamboyant, boastful brother Frederick, who channels the reckless "bad boy" archetype, Henry offers a model of enlightened masculinity. He gently teases Catherine about her fascination with Gothic novels – telling her, "You are a very clever, sensible girl and I am quite convinced that you will find no ghosts at Northanger Abbey" [9] – but his humour is never cruel. Rather, he encourages her to balance imagination with reason, urging her to "consult your own understanding, your own sense of the probable,"[10] and thus navigate the gap between fantasy and reality. Meanwhile, John Thorpe serves as a sharp foil: loud, self-important and manipulative, he embodies the kind of opportunistic and superficial masculinity that Gothic heroines often must beware of. Through these contrasting male figures, Austen not only engages with Gothic character types but also explores different models of male behaviour in relation to female agency, imagination and social expectations. Henry's respectful support and intellectual companionship mark him as a progressive force within this landscape, guiding Catherine toward a more mature and grounded understanding of herself and the world.

While *Northanger Abbey* remains Austen's most overt engagement with the Gothic, subtle genre influences ripple throughout her other novels. These echoes appear less as direct parodies and more as nuanced elements woven into settings, characterisations and plotlines. By incorporating the familiar genre elements in varied and often understated ways, Austen explores the tensions between fantasy and reality, passion and reason, and youthful imagination and mature insight, all whilst

---

9 Austen, Jane. Chapter 25. *Northanger Abbey.*
10 Austen, Jane. Chapter 24. *Northanger Abbey.*

maintaining an ongoing conversation with the genre's hallmarks.

Marianne Dashwood in *Sense and Sensibility* (1811) emerges as a character shaped by Romantic and darkly sensational ideals. Her heightened romantic desires and emotions recall those heroines undone by passion. For instance, Marianne is caught in, not one, but two rainstorms and rescued each time – first by the dashing Willoughby, a fantasy figure aligned with the archetypal villain of Romantic melodrama and later by the grounded Colonel Brandon, a more realistic and moral counterpart. Her near-fatal illness after Willoughby's rejection also echoes the suffering common in sentimental and supernatural tales, where female characters are emotionally and physically endangered by failed love. Yet Austen rejects the tragic outcomes typical of these narratives, allowing Marianne to recover.

Even in *Pride and Prejudice* (1813), a novel often anchored in social realism, faint echoes of the Gothic surface. Elizabeth Bennet's first view of Pemberley is loaded with emotional intensity and awe, almost like the moment a Gothic heroine enters a mysterious ancestral home. Darcy himself could be seen as a brooding, Byronic figure – misunderstood and emotionally reserved – although Austen eventually reshapes him into a figure of moral clarity. Lady Catherine de Bourgh can also be considered alongside other fictional tyrants such as authoritarian fathers or manipulative abbesses: she's a powerful, domineering figure who seeks to control young lovers' futures.

Taking a more playful approach, *Emma* (1815) allows the Gothic to survive chiefly within the heroine's imagination. Emma Woodhouse, like Catherine Morland, misreads social situations through the lens of fantasy. Her romantic speculation about Frank Churchill and Jane Fairfax plays into the genre's fondness for hidden identities and secret engagements. Frank, charming and manipulative, resembles the deceptive Gothic suitor – although Austen ultimately contains the danger through comic resolution. Emma's imaginative meddling extends to Harriet Smith, whose humble background she recasts in fanciful terms, believing her to be the unacknowledged daughter of genteel or even noble parentage. This desire to elevate Harriet echoes the Gothic fascination with mysterious origins and secret inheritances. In both cases, Emma's projections reveal the dangers of mistaking social performance for emotional truth – a more subtle version of the genre's obsession with disguise and deception.

Far more sustained in its Gothic overtones, *Mansfield Park* (1814) presented some of Austen's darkest imagery. Sotherton Court, with its locked gates, crumbling chapel and morally ambiguous landscape, evokes the haunted estates of Radcliffean fiction. The garden scene, in which Maria Bertram slips through a gate with Henry Crawford, hints at transgression – both literal and symbolic.

Finally, in *Persuasion* (1818), Austen leaned more deeply into Romantic and atmospheric elements than anywhere else in her oeuvre. The trip to Lyme Regis introduces a dramatic setting of sea cliffs, storms and dangerous falls, most vividly realised in Louisa Musgrove's accident on the Cobb. This episode evokes the sublime landscapes typical of dark romantic fiction and introduces a rare moment of physical jeopardy. Anne Elliot, the novel's heroine, is haunted not by ghosts but by memory and loss. Captain Wentworth's return from the sea, once thought lost to her, carries the emotional intensity of a resurrection. The theme of reunion after separation aligns with the Gothic's enduring fascination with death, return and the tension between past and present.

Though Austen's later works engage with Gothic motifs more subtly, she does not discard them altogether, but rather distils their themes – shifting the drama from haunted castles to drawing rooms, from overt peril to internal tension. This quiet transformation enriched her narrative worlds and deepens her exploration of character, morality and misapprehension.

This interplay between Austen's realism and darker romantic sensibilities has not only deepened scholarly appreciation but also helped to sustain her cultural legacy. From 20th- and 21st-century film and television adaptations to playful genre mash-ups, Austen's engagement with heightened narrative conventions continues to inspire reinvention. Ang Lee's *Sense and Sensibility* (1995), adapted by and starring Emma Thompson, vividly captures this mood. One striking moment features Marianne Dashwood (Kate Winslet) collapsing in a rain-soaked field, only to be swept up by the dashing John Willoughby (Greg Wise), his sharp sideburns and billowing cloak evoking the quintessential Byronic hero. The scene channels romantic melodrama – peril, sublime landscape and male rescue – yet Austen ultimately subverts the fantasy by exposing Willoughby's unreliability and emotional cowardice. The film highlights both the allure and the danger of romantic excess, underscoring Austen's layered critique.

Other pastiche novels like *Pride and Prejudice and Zombies* (2009, Seth Grahame-Smith), *Sense and Sensibility and Sea Monsters* (2009, Ben H. Winters) and *Vampire Darcy's Desire* (2010, Regina Jeffers) blend Austen's historical settings with supernatural elements, creating postmodern homages to the genre she so deftly parodied, ensuring her continued relevance across audiences and media.

Throughout her novels, Austen consistently engaged with Gothic conventions – not merely to parody them, but to adapt and refine them. Whether through brooding figures, dangerous estates, emotional intensity or social misreadings, she recasts Gothic tropes in the service of psychological realism. She retained the genre's fascination with mystery and feeling, but strips away its excesses, transforming a literature of fear into one of insight and irony.

Jane Austen and the Gothic Novel

Ellen Cheshire holds an MA in Gothic: Culture, Subculture, Counterculture from St Mary's University and a BA (Hons) in Humanities: Film and English from the University of North London.

Over the past 25 years, Ellen has published widely in journals, books, magazines and British Film Institute publications. Ellen has written books on Jane Campion and Ang Lee for Supernova's *In the Scene* series and contributed to their anthologies *Counterculture UK: A Celebration* and *Silent: Women Pioneers of Cinema,* and worked on archive projects for Taschen and educational texts for Hodder Education. Alongside writing, Ellen teaches film and has a background in arts and media management.

Love's Armour

Allyson Joule

Love came at me
like a seasoned boxer,
landing blows
I didn't see coming.
I stood there,
open-chested,
thinking tenderness
would be enough armour.
Now I carry the
ache in my ribs,
each breath
a memory
of the fight.

Love's Armour

Allyson Joule is a romance poet and novelist. A native of Dallas, Texas, she began writing poetry and narrative stories at a young age and her work has been featured in magazines, poetry slams, and web collaborations. Her first poetry book *Shattered: Poems for the Brokenhearted* is described as "a deeply moving exploration of the highs and lows of unrequited love." Her first paranormal romance novel and her second poetry collection are coming out in early 2026. allysonjoule.com.

The Completion Competition

Natalie Jenner

"Those who tell their own story, you know, must be listened to with caution."
— Jane Austen, *Sanditon*

Chawton Cottage
March 1817

She always entered the parlour with the sun.

This was her time, contained by one hundred revolutions on the grandfather clock. One hundred minutes to get Charlotte Heywood in front of a seaside stranger and capture his heart. Would class distinction separate them from the start? Poverty could be the death-knell to romantic inclination, as well as a perfect way to wind up the plot. Look at Darcy and Elizabeth, before romance won out.

"Morning, miss – may I stoke the fire for you?"

She started at the voice, her mind already in Sanditon.

"Thank you, William." She took the tea caddy down from its perch in the cupboard next to the hearth and peered inside. There was enough tea for now, but a trip to London and Twinings would soon be in order – if her health allowed.

William waited in the doorway as she replaced the caddy and crossed the hearth to the small pedestal table. Its smooth octagonal surface was just large enough for her tools, and the

The Completion Competition

nearby window gave her a view of the world – a small world of dustmen and washerwomen and coaches passing through, but an entire universe for her. She sat down and lifted the quill pen, and still William waited.

She stared out the window at the bleak sky, the constant drizzle masking any sign of spring. The pang in her side was insistent, lessened only by the writing. She was grateful for this ability to build something, however clay-like it remained in her hands. She could play with it or pinch it depending on her mood. Without such pliability of thought, she feared turning into her mother, venom directed outwards instead of in. Writing, like life, must never look too far ahead.

Charlotte had been ten days at Sanditon without seeing Sanditon House.

But she could see it. She could see it as if it was situated at the end of the lane before her. The grandest house for Lady Denham that her imagination could design, with rooms baroque in décor and gilded in gold, everything done to excess, everything shouting out to anyone who crossed the threshold that here resided power. How she loved a powerful widow. She wished her sister Cassandra possessed such stature, instead of the small allowance left by her late fiancé. But at least he had left her something. At least she had been *left*.

The words started to pour forth with the anchor of the made-up house. She only needed to know a place to populate it. She had learnt many such lessons from her novels, duty to the reader being paramount above all. Everything – every sentence, every notion, every descriptive word – must be in service to the story.

She enjoyed the presence of William in the parlour as she wrote in the small booklet before her. The sound of his labours always soothed her mind. Already this morning the young footman had brought in milk from the Great House stables and wood for the fire that began to warm her aching back. When he joined the household last summer, both she and Cassandra had noted his strong features and pleasant manner. Later, following not insignificant mental exertion upon hearing the news, the sisters reconciled themselves to the fact that William's aunt had acted as their own village wet nurse – the first time they had been sent away from home too young. In a family full of boys, she and Cassie were often left to each other, a state forced upon them in childhood which they wielded in spinsterhood to great effect. Together, they could be quite terrifying.

She laid down her quill pen, having reached the perfect moment to pause. She needed to let the words alone for a bit, to settle on the page like soot. Needed for the pain to subside.

*

He was hesitant to make a sound until she was well in her head without him. She would keep the quill pen upright in her hand, gaze out the window, crease her brow. There would be a breath – deeper than the rest – before she would start, followed by a dip of the pen in ink. And then silence, just the scratching of the quill end as it scurried across the page.

But the staring out the window was taking longer of late, the breath more laboured. He was worried. She held so much in her head and in her hands, the entire household it seemed. She asked little of others and hardly anything of him, a lowly footman; just the silence he could give her, and the stories. She left the house less and less, and he was proud to bring her the gossip he heard in the lane and at the pub. It was the least he could do.

He couldn't read her own stories, although he knew by now of their fame. But he did his best to catch the lines she occasionally threw out like lures. He couldn't see past the words to the woman at the table, a woman whose world grew smaller by the day. Couldn't see the other ladies of the house or the

The Completion Competition

many friends and relations who came to visit. He gave her the real-life tidings from Chawton and these, too, disappeared on the page. Or became something else. Something better.

The scratching slowed down. He waited, his back tight with worry, minutes it seemed. The scratching on the page became the rain on the pane, drizzling down to nothing. The grandfather clock ticked its sombre march of time, the only sound now in the room. And still he waited, for as long as he could bear.

*

"Miss?" William sat back on his heels, looking up at her in concern. "I'm sorry to speak, miss, but are you alright?"

The question surprised her; the servants knew never to address her during this time. She wondered how long she had been sitting there, not writing. She was *not* writing more and more of late.

"Yes, William. Perfectly alright. Thank you."

He returned to stoking the fire that would soon brown the toast for breakfast and heat the water for tea. So many natural elements were at play in the room: the darting flames, the windows wet with rain, the new sun struggling to break through. This was her favourite time to write: the mind clear of the mundane, the spirit energised by sleep. But the magic had been broken by the pain today, and the pen stayed down.

"William, did you run into anyone this morning on your walk?"

She knew this was all the invitation he needed, and he straightened himself with a smile.

"No one in particular, miss – that is, just the ladies Fitzgerald fussing over their new pony cart. The way them two fuss over the animals and cut each other down with dread... I'd be willing to venture they'd give the other up, if it'd mean a

Encounters with Jane Austen

new collection of hounds to keep 'em company instead."

She smiled back as he shared the village gossip. She loved the cadence of his voice, the rhyming of his sentences, all the while the speaker himself so blissfully unaware of both effort and result. She wanted a character in her new story to speak this way – a truth-teller, like Thomas in *Sense and Sensibility*, first to tell the Dashwood family that Mr Ferrars is married. Station in life would not matter – who *was* he to be? She could make him anything: a vegetable farmer, a barrister, a thief. After the landed gentry of Pemberley, Mansfield Park, and Highbury, she wanted to widen the range of possible suitors for a heroine like Miss Heywood. Class distinction or not, they were both running out of time.

She turned back to her work as William finished with the fire, standing to brush the soot from his knees with his large, capable hands. He was tall, as tall as the six-foot-high clock by the hearth, and wore the striped shirt the family had gifted him at Christmas. They had all stood together that festive morning in the parlour, the servants and the four women of the house: she and Cassandra, their mother, dear friend Martha Lloyd. It had been a short exchange, thrown into relief by the much more extravagant gathering a few hours later at the Great House where older brother Edward resided. Edward always did like to enjoy himself to excess.

William left the parlour and she returned to the brothers on the page. Sidney Parker was about to enter Sanditon from the misty brow of the hill – another perfect place to pause. She had added her five hundred words for the day. When it came to her writing, she was a creature of habit but never of superstition – there was no room for *that* when trying to tell a story. A better word for it was 'practiced,' like the muscles that lifted her fingers on the pianoforte as if with a will of their own. She had been doing this for thirty years, after all.

There was a noise from the road outside the window,

The Completion Competition

like the low rumbling before a storm, joined by the echoing clip-clopping of horses approaching closer. She put her pen back down in surprise at the early arrival from Alton of the Winchester coach. Louisa Cooper, her second-youngest cousin on her mother's side, had not been expected until after breakfast. She pushed the booklet beneath the blotting paper – there would be no more writing today.

William quickly passed through the parlour again, surprised himself by the sudden appearance of that month's guest. Soon Louisa could be heard laughing at something in the front hall while William walked back and forth from the road, bringing in her trunk and many parcels, uttering not a word for all of Louisa's attempts at conversation.

"I know it's horrid of me to arrive so early like this" she heard the girl say. "I deserve a real set-down for disturbing you both."

From her seat by the window, she felt her jaw tighten. Such girlish vivacity – and interruption of her writing – lately set her teeth on edge. This, even though seventeen-year-old Louisa was goodhearted enough and slyly playful, making her a favourite among them. Placing the cap on the inkwell, she stood up from the table and came forward to hug her cousin as she entered the parlour.

"My dear, you look well. A nice flush to the cheeks." She looked past Louisa at William standing stock-still in the hall behind her, his own face slightly reddened. The trunk was at his feet and Miss Heywood's – Louisa's, that is – many packages had been piled high on top. "Shall we leave Miss Cooper's things for later?"

William gave a curt nod and headed for the back staircase. Louisa watched him leave before turning to her with a frown.

"He never talks."

"He most certainly does."

"Well, he's never spoken a word to me." Louisa removed her gloves and coat and tossed them onto a nearby chair. "Were you writing just now?"

"A little."

"A little," Louisa repeated with a laugh. "Not one of your many letters? A new story perhaps?"

The young woman's tone – lazy with presumption – set off something else inside her. "You just had my Emma, you know."

Louisa hesitated, then made a face all too recognisable. "Yes. But we are always eager for more."

The pain was back, this time radiating to her other side. Sharper – *much* sharper. She reached for the edge of the dining table to steady herself.

"Oh, cousin Jane… here, please, do sit. I will put the water on for us."

The young woman busied herself about the hearth, moving with such ease. Everything hurt – even just to watch her. In a life marked mostly by comings and goings, the pain was her constant companion now.

*

But why did she have to be so suspicious about it all? Louisa asked herself as she placed the kettle on the grate.

There were so many unspoken rules about the writing: when it was to be done, when to interrupt, even when to laugh. Jane would never express pride in her authorship out loud, but it was written on her face – and why ever not? Some might consider the writing just one more feminine pursuit, however brilliantly done, yet Sir Walter Scott and even the Prince Regent read the novels.

But the pride also finished off the edges of Jane's sharp

The Completion Competition

intellect and left her prickly. Only with cousin Cassandra did Jane exhibit a constant desire to please. Yet despite the sisters' great intimacy, Louisa felt sorry for them both: the failed romances, the rejected proposals, the lovers lost at sea. Perhaps the writing was to fault. If Jane saw everything through the lens of her talent – her genius, the family declared – how could daily life ever measure up?

Worse, what if the magic in her pen were to one day suddenly stop? For it must be magic, given the ease and regularity with which the words poured forth and the stories took shape. Louisa herself had endless ideas to write up, but always relinquished these to any invitations that might secure her future as a bride. There would be plenty of time to write later, should she marry well.

Had Jane in her youth been as serious about writing as she was today, when all such invitations for her had long since dried up? Or had the seriousness come with the disappointed heart of middle age? All Louisa knew was that ever since the move to Chawton cottage, the rest of the household was to steer clear of the dining parlour until breakfast at nine – only Mrs Austen's new footman appeared to enjoy special dispensation. Jane's efforts during those early hours remained as mysterious as her talent, as hidden as the workings of her mind. *This was the marriage in Jane's life,* said Louisa to herself, *the union between a great intellect cultivated by circumstance and the gift of genius from God above.* Oh, she did like the sound of that. She must remember to write it down, when next there was time.

*

"Are you sharing yet?" Louisa had settled herself at the dining table and was arranging tea. On the small eight-sided table by the window, Sidney Parker stayed hidden in the mist.

"You know I don't share anything ahead of its time. Especially not a story."

Encounters with Jane Austen

But it would be different with this one, although she would never say that aloud. She was trying to pin enough down before it was too late. She had completed "The Elliots" last summer under similarly trying circumstances, but always in the hope that her health would somehow improve with time. In this new year, her body continued to challenge and fail her – lately she feared her spirits were failing it in turn.

"How is your own writing progressing?" she asked Louisa, due less to interest than evasion. In dark times like this, she saw the writerly ambitions of her many cousins, nieces, and nephews as leech-like, trying to draw from her own depleting stores of energy. What would they all do, the lot of them, when she was gone? What stories might they write about her?

In a family full of aspiring writers, she was the visionary – she stood alone. She had always known of this singular power, even though she would never dare give voice to it – not to anyone, not even Cassie. The knowledge stayed inside her and would die with her; the power increased with the pain. Pain which stripped away at life, leaving her facing nothing but an ending that everyone else refused to see. Still, she could ready herself – and them – for the journey; she could choose what to leave behind. Surely the start of a story was, in a family like theirs, the most apt legacy of all.

A *competition,* she suddenly thought to herself as Louisa chattered on. *A competition to complete "The Brothers."*

The pain in her side eased momentarily under the wonder of this thought. Who knew if the earlier books 'By A Lady' would survive her – the reading public was fickle enough with the living. And the letters, in agreement with her sister, were to be burned. One day everyone that read her would be gone. Would her stories go with them, too?

She had filled only two booklets with this new story, when completion should take at least ten. The manuscript could easily end up relegated among the papers to be destroyed. But

The Completion Competition

if she shared the story soon, it might light a spark amongst a family whose competitiveness with each other – from play-acting and sermons to college and the navy – rarely abated.

They all enjoyed word games and riddles in verse; her mother even wrote recipes in rhyme. Eldest brother James had fancied himself a poet until the clergy; Henry, her favourite, had dabbled in fiction at college. Henry did like to try his hand at so many things. Perhaps young cousin Louisa would take up the torch – Louisa whose gifts in life included time and education, each essential for talent to take flight. But preoccupation with the self kept Louisa's imagination rooted to the ground.

She would have selected William to finish the story, natural teller of tales as he was, but he could not read or write. In fact, he had not been given a day of schooling in his life. She recalled her own childhood, the moment as a toddler when the shapes on the page first matched the sounds of her rector father's voice (*"No child has ever read so young!"* he had boasted long after, and nothing had made her more proud). She had grown up practically tripping over books.

"I simply can't seem to get started. I have too many ideas, I suppose," Louisa answered with an easy laugh.

She smiled at the unintentional truth. "Starting has never been the difficulty for me."

This was also the truth. For with each new start, there had been hope – the very reason for the writing. How the heart soared with every new brick laid in the made-up great houses, every cutting remark that put someone deservedly in their place, every happy ending built from shapeless clay into a fortress against the future.

Hers had been a life, in fact, full of beginnings – new homes, new potential suitors to meet, new books to write. But the climax had never come, after all.

For that, she had had to write her books.

Encounters with Jane Austen

Photo:Sara Sims

Natalie Jenner is the internationally and number one nationally bestselling author of *The Jane Austen Society, Bloomsbury Girls, Every Time We Say Goodbye,* and *Austen at Sea,* which have been translated into more than twenty languages worldwide. Her non-fiction writing on Jane Austen includes essays in *Literary Hub* and *Paste* magazine, as well as introductions to the Plumleaf Press editions of *Lady Susan* and *Pride and Prejudice.*

Natalie graduated from the University of Toronto with consecutive degrees in English literature and law, and previously has worked as a corporate lawyer, career coach, and independent bookshop proprietor. Currently an ambassador for the Jane Austen Literacy Foundation, Natalie was born in England and raised in Ontario, Canada, where she lives with her family and two rescue dogs.

Mr Bingley and Mr Darcy

Austen's Onscreen Evolution

From Faithful Adaptations to Playful Interpretations

Jen Francis

Jane Austen's first novel, *Sense and Sensibility*, was published in 1811. Over a century later, in 1938, the first screen adaptation of her work – a televised version of *Pride and Prejudice* – aired on the BBC. And that was only the beginning. Across countries, languages, and decades, Austen's novels have found favour on screen, evolving with each generation while continuing to draw audiences in.

There are still those who dismiss the validity of these adaptations – faithful Austenites who argue that no screen version can capture the richness of her characterisation or the subtlety of her prose. But there's a strong argument that it's these very adaptations keeping Austen's stories in the minds (and feeds) of younger generations. In an age when Gen Z and Gen Alpha are reading less fiction and spending more time on streaming platforms and social media, the screen has become a powerful gateway into classic literature.

And so, Austen's stories have been kept on their toes. With screen usage shifting from scheduled programming to on-demand content, and with platforms like Netflix and YouTube reshaping how stories are consumed, her Regency origins have been reframed to fit contemporary formats. Yet despite the aesthetic updates, the heart of Austen's work remains firmly intact.

Austen's Onscreen Evolution

Centring themes of love (*Pride and Prejudice*), class (*Emma*), social mobility (*Sense and Sensibility*), and self-discovery (*Persuasion*) – these are stories where, rather than being relegated to the sidelines, women take centre stage in their own lives. It's a truth universally acknowledged that these themes still resonate with the wants and needs of many modern audiences.

And it's not just about how these stories are told, but where. With attention spans decreasing and screen sizes shrinking, for Austen's words to continue reaching new audiences around the world, they've had to travel – from page to screen, from classrooms to algorithms. And somehow, in all their forms, they still connect.

The average film runs for around 120 minutes. A television series, on the other hand, can stretch to 700 minutes or more. That's nearly six times the length – and therein lies the key benefit of a television adaptation over a film adaptation. Television gives Austen's works the time and space they need to breathe, to linger in quiet moments, and to fully expand their emotional and narrative complexity.

A key example is *Sense and Sensibility*. Austen's first novel, which follows the changing fortunes and romantic entanglements of sisters Elinor and Marianne, and was first adapted into a feature film in 1995. Scripted by Emma Thompson (who also stars as the dutiful Elinor Dashwood) and directed by Ang Lee, the film is widely admired – but with just 136 minutes to work with, adjustments had to be made. Several minor characters, such as Miss Steele, Lady Middleton, and John Dashwood's son, are omitted. These characters provide texture and help flesh out the social world of the novel, but in a film with a limited runtime, they're trimmed to streamline the plot.

Beyond characters, whole subplots and emotional arcs are condensed. Brandon's quiet love for Marianne is underplayed, Edward and Elinor's relationship is sped up, and Marianne's poetic sensibility – a key part of her emotional journey – is touched on but not deeply explored. Perhaps most notably, Willoughby's lengthy and complex confession is skipped entirely, replaced with a silent moment of regret from afar. It works for the pacing of the film but what it inevitably loses is the depth and the clarity which can be found in the novel.

This is where the 2008 BBC series excels. Though not as celebrated as the film, it is respected for its authenticity – keeping much of Austen's language and dialogue and allowing space for quieter moments to shine. The romantic tension between Edward and Elinor builds gradually, with restraint and subtlety. Willoughby's confession is included, giving viewers a deeper understanding of his character. Brandon's devotion is given time to grow on screen, and Marianne's transformation from impulsive romantic to more grounded young woman feels earned.

This pattern – of omission, compression, or amplification – can also be seen in other adaptations, such as *Mansfield Park*. The 2007 ITV film version, starring Billie Piper, simplifies the story to suit a 90-minute runtime, but in doing so, loses much of Fanny Price's internal complexity. Meanwhile, longer TV versions (such as the 1983 adaptation) afford more time to explore themes of moral integrity, self-worth, and familial tension – just as they are highlighted in the novel. For example, despite his questionable character, Fanny is pressured by her family to accept Henry as a husband because of his wealth. In the series, Fanny's refusal is a powerful act of defiance due to her own destituteness and the fact that marrying Henry would mean she is no longer treated like a second class citizen by the Bertrams – particularly, Aunt Norris.

Fanny knows herself. She knows what she wants. In the film, Fanny's attraction to Edmund feels like childish infatuation due to the compression of time. In the series, however, there is room for subtlety and nuance as Fanny slowly realises the love she has for her cousin. The audience also has time to see Edmund's point of view and believe his eventual realisation of Fanny's worth which has been evident all along.

BBC and ITV have adapted Austen's works like it's their part-time job. From the 1970s onwards, they've been responsible for dozens of television adaptations, shaping how a number of generations visualise Austen's world. From the Bennet Sisters to less popularised heroines like Northanger Abbey's, Catherine Morland, they've brought her characters into the cultural mainstream. This has done more than keep Austen relevant – it has been instrumental in defining period drama itself.

Though traditional weekly TV viewing has given way to streaming and bingeing, there's still something to be said for the communal experience of sinking one's teeth into a six-part series. That format – six one-hour episodes – has become the gold standard for classic Austen retellings. It's the model that best mirrors the experience of reading her novels: steady, immersive, and full of detail. It may not match Austen word for word, but it gets closer to the real thing.

While there's often an expectation of faithfulness to the original when it comes to Austen adaptations, reinterpretations i.e. the looser, more playful kind – have found widespread success across generations and continents. They may not be faithful in structure or dialogue, but they tap into something more essential: Austen's spirit.

Clueless (1995) is perhaps the most beloved example. The film centres on Cher Horowitz (Alicia Silverstone), a stylish, wealthy teenager living in Beverly Hills who fancies herself a matchmaker. Her latest project is Tai (Brittany Murphy), a new student in need of a makeover – but, of course, Cher's meddling doesn't go to plan. The idea of mapping Austen's handsome, clever and rich Emma Woodhouse onto a 'ditzy' 90s high school queen bee shouldn't work – but it does.

Encounters with Jane Austen

Clueless is smart, funny, and full of heart. Like Emma, Cher learns that good intentions don't excuse ignorance, and self-awareness doesn't always come easy. The societal expectations and balls may be swapped for school cliques and malls, but the characters and emotional arcs remain firmly Austenian.

Fast forward six years and *Bridget Jones's Diary* (2001) brings another modern Austen heroine to the screen. Bridget (Renée Zellweger) is a thirty-something Londoner caught between two men: Mark Darcy (Colin Firth), the uptight, seemingly disinterested barrister, and Daniel Cleaver (Hugh Grant), Bridget's charismatic but unreliable boss. If this sounds familiar that's because it is. Loosely based on *Pride and Prejudice*, the film reworks Elizabeth Bennet's romantic dilemma into something messier, more neurotic, and undeniably early-2000s. Bridget is awkward, insecure, and drinks too much Chardonnay – but like Lizzy, she's sharp, (*eventually*) self-reflective, and ultimately discovers that first impressions can be misleading.

Other adaptations lean even further into creative license. *Scents and Sensibility* (2011) transplants the Dashwood sisters into modern-day Utah, where they launch a homemade lotion business after their father's arrest. *From Prada to Nada* (2011) shifts the action to East LA, turning Austen's tale of wealth and inheritance into a story about cultural identity and economic hardship in a Latinx community. These may not be polished period dramas, but they carry Austen's reoccurring themes of resilience, family, and reinvention.

These kinds of adaptations pose an interesting question: how much of Austen's novels can you restructure or change before they stop being Austen? Is it the characters, the setting, the dialogue – or is it something deeper? Perhaps it's the themes that matter most: female autonomy, personal growth, a love that is earned, and a sharp wit to survive whatever life – or your family – throws at you.

Maybe its because reinterpretations take such creative

liberties that they aren't judged as harshly as traditional adaptations. When a film cuts minor characters for time, it's a betrayal. When a reinterpretation swaps corsets for crop tops, it's innovation.

These modern retellings have become cultural touchstones – whether you're a Valley Girl or a British singleton, the emotional truths still land. It might not be widely known that *Clueless* is *Emma*, or that Bridget owes a debt to Lizzy Bennet, but these films are living proof that Austen continues to resonate – no matter how you wrap her up.

We've explored classic Austen and modern interpretations, but there's a fascinating middle ground emerging – adaptations that retain period settings but update the tone, aesthetic, or delivery for younger audiences. These versions toe the line between reverence and reinvention, often with polarising results.

Take *Emma* (2020), starring Anya Taylor-Joy. The film was widely praised for its striking, almost painterly visuals – crisp, oversaturated, and symmetrical – with an ensemble cast that leant into the absurdities of high society. But for all its style, the portrayal of Emma herself divided opinion. In the novel, Emma is "handsome, clever and rich," yes, but also spoiled with good intentions. She's misguided, not malicious. While the 1996 and 2009 adaptations preserve that careful balance, the 2020 version amped up her aloofness to the point where she felt more like a fashion-forward mean girl than a flawed but lovable matchmaker. The snark was there, but the softness wasn't – and without that, much of her charm was lost. In trying to spoon feed an insta-ready audience, the film forgot that you can't root for someone if you don't like them.

Another recent Austen with a generational lens is *Persuasion* (2022), produced by Netflix and starring Dakota Johnson. Here, Anne Elliot – typically introverted, quiet, and contemplative – is reimagined as a wry, fourth-wall-breaking heroine with the

Encounters with Jane Austen

sharp tongue and self-deprecating wit of a Londoner who'd moved to the country and instantly regretted it. She drinks wine straight from the bottle, cuddles rabbits, and makes jokes about exes like she's in a Regency rom-com. The intention was clear: make Anne relatable. The result? A deeply jarring clash between Austen's world and Fleabag-esque narration. Critics were quick to condemn the modernised language, with lines like "He's a ten – I never trust a ten," feeling more like Twitter drafts than 19th-century reflection. Despite its failings, though, the film did spark conversation and drew curious viewers to Austen's final completed novel – many of whom may never have read it otherwise.

A better balance was struck in *Sanditon* (2019–2023), a series inspired by Austen's unfinished novel. Created by Andrew Davies (of *Pride and Prejudice* 1995 fame), *Sanditon* blends traditional Regency drama with bolder storytelling. It features the familiar Austen beats – witty heroines, brooding suitors, social scheming – but also takes creative liberties, introducing interracial romances, commercial ambition, and slightly steamier storylines. Though not without controversy, *Sanditon* managed to modernise Austen's world without completely warping it, proving there's space for innovation within historical constraints.

The passion behind these adaptations is clear. Over 200 years later, people still want to engage with Austen's words – to repackage, restyle and reintroduce them to the world. But in doing so, they walk a tightrope. On one side is reliability, on the other, relatability. Tip too far either way and you risk alienating both loyal fans and potential newcomers.

Still, in a crowded streaming landscape, even the most divisive Austen adaptations tend to draw eyes. For better or for worse, one could argue that what matters most is that Austen remains part of the ever evolving conversation.

If *Pride and Prejudice* is the British *Little Women*, then Elizabeth

Austen's Onscreen Evolution

Bennet is our Jo March – layered, compelling, independent, and a star-making role for whoever dares step into her boots. The novel remains the most adapted of Austen's works – with good reason. It is the blueprint for romantic tension, witty repartee, and biting social commentary. And with each new version, new generations are drawn into the familiar and exciting rhythm of Darcy's pride meeting Elizabeth's prejudice.

Two of the most debated adaptations – the BBC's 1995 series starring Jennifer Ehle and Colin Firth, and Joe Wright's 2005 film starring Keira Knightley and Matthew Macfadyen – stand as proof that tone, aesthetic, and performance shape how Austen is interpreted and remembered. The 1995 version leans into slow-burn storytelling. As a television adaptation it affords viewers the luxury of time: of meaningful glances, tense silences, and carefully drawn supporting characters. Colin Firth's Darcy became the definitive version – so much so that his infamous "wet shirt" scene, became forever stitched into British pop culture.

By contrast, the 2005 film is moodier and more cinematic. Misty fields and candlelit interiors capture a younger, more emotionally raw Elizabeth and a far broodier, bordering on awkward, Darcy. Though more condensed, it doesn't lack for tension. Macfadyen's clenching hand has spawned its own wave of discourse which solidifies the beauty of Austen's world. One which continues to invite conversation and interpretation, no matter its form.

Even bolder takes of Austen's most popular text exists. *Pride and Prejudice and Zombies* (2016) places Elizabeth in a dystopian England, sword-fighting the undead while still dodging Mr. Collins. It's absurd, yes, but still fundamentally about survival, sisterhood, and those unavoidable societal expectations – all hallmarks of Austen's key themes. Meanwhile, *The Lizzie Bennet Diaries*, a YouTube vlog-style retelling, gave Austen fans of 2012 a modern Elizabeth – Lizzie – navigating grad school, family drama, and romance via social media. By letting Lizzie speak directly to the camera, the series connected with a digital generation without diluting Austen's core messages.

Pride and Prejudice is not just Austen's most adapted work – it's her most malleable and Elizabeth Bennet and Fitzwilliam Darcy remain like friends. Whether in regency attire or wielding a katana, Elizabeth remains the heroine we get mad at but ultimately root for, and Darcy, the enigma we long to both shake and comfort.

Though Jane Austen wrote about a very particular world – white, upper-middle-class Regency England – her stories have long since outgrown those narrow lanes. Across continents and cultures, her themes of love, family, class, and societal pressure have proven strikingly universal. In fact, the very things that seem most "British" about Austen – the rigid social hierarchy, the silent judgments at dinner parties, the coded language of romance – are easily recognisable in many parts of the world.

Take *Bride and Prejudice* (2004), a Bollywood musical directed by Gurinder Chadha. In it, Austen's story of love, misjudgement, and pride unfolds in India and London, complete with elaborate dance numbers, cultural clashes, and mothers who are inevitably desperate to see their daughters married. The core conflict between independent-minded Lalita (Elizabeth) and snobbish Will Darcy remains, but it's reframed through the lens of postcolonial identity and globalisation. In this context, Darcy's ignorance isn't just class-based – it's cultural.

Similarly, *Aisha* (2010), an Indian take on *Emma*, sets Austen's meddling heroine against the backdrop of Delhi's elite. While Aisha shops for handbags, the essence of Austen's character – well-meaning but blinkered – remains untouched. And *From Prada to Nada* (2011), a Latinx reimagining of *Sense and Sensibility*, trades rural cottages for East LA but keeps its focus on two sisters navigating economic hardship and emotional upheaval.

Austen's Onscreen Evolution

These adaptations don't just transplant Austen's characters into new settings – they underscore how adaptable her values are. Love across social boundaries, the friction between tradition and personal choice, the yearning for freedom as a woman – these are not British problems, they're human ones.

Even when Austen isn't being directly referenced, her influence lingers. Korean dramas frequently draw on her archetypes: the misunderstood wealthy suitor, the heroine who refuses to bow to social pressure, the meddling families. Austen's DNA is embedded in global romance storytelling, whether credited or not.

By moving Austen's stories into diverse cultures and languages, international adaptations often inject a freshness that UK retellings can sometimes lack. They challenge assumptions about Austen's work being 'quaint' or 'outdated' and prove that her stories are still relevant – whether set in Bath or Bangkok.

Jane Austen's stories have proven infinitely adaptable – more than 200 years on, filmmakers, writers, and audiences are still finding new ways to explore her wit, warmth, and wisdom. From faithful BBC adaptations to zombie mash-ups, from YouTube vloggers to Bollywood musical numbers, her characters have danced through almost every genre and format imaginable.

And yet, the debate continues: do we honour Austen best through strict text to screen adaptations or through bold reinvention? The purists crave textual authenticity; the progressives argue that reinterpretation keeps her work alive. Perhaps both are right. Austen's enduring legacy lies not just in how we retell her stories but in why we keep coming back to them.

Because in the end, her work speaks to something timeless – the search for love, the desire to be understood and the courage to defy expectations. Whether it's a six-part BBC miniseries that ticks all those British Period Drama boxes or a TikTok musical (not yet – but let's be honest, entirely possible), Austen's world continues to offer a mirror to society as it infinitely reflects our world through her eyes – and her pen.

Jen Francis is a freelance TV producer director, film writer and podcaster. She has over a decade of experience in the creative industries and is the author of the film guide *In The Scene: Steve McQueen* (Supernova Books).

Shedding Skin

Jurie Jean van de Vyver

When the morning breaks,
take me back to the earth.
A chorus of birds dapples
this dawn of expectation.
Possibility spills into shadow
as the sun greets green
and brown and blue
and you and I.

When the bells ring,
take me back to the earth.
Walk with me into the house of service
to remember
that time falls like raindrops
and that space is a medium
to experience love becoming
love becoming
love.

When the drought comes,
take me back to the earth.
Remind me what thirst is for,

Encounters with Jane Austen

and to hold my nerve
until the butterflies come:
harbingers of the journeys
of those who flew before
and those who fly ahead.

When the rain comes,
take me back to the earth.
Quench this yearning thirst:
a seeking sustained through glimpses
of losing oneself
to the space between.
Giving and receiving,
receiving and giving.

When the storm breaks,
take me back to the earth.
Allow me to let me go,
fully,
as the waves and lightning
make my smallness known.
Adrift in this vulnerable boat,
I pray,
I pray.

When the celebration comes,
take me back to the earth.
A feast of plenty
made with love,

Shedding Skin

weaving together
those who are here
and those who aren't.

When the evening beckons,
take me back to the earth.
Turquoise blue and glistening gold,
you bid farewell.
The lapping waves bring news
of butterflies
and tectonic plates.

When my time comes,
take me back to the earth.
A labyrinth walked
among mountains
and forests
and rivers,
all alive.
Again and again
and again.

Encounters with Jane Austen

Jurie Jean van de Vyver is a systems thinker, environmentalist and organisational leadership advisor. He is a certified Chartered Accountant (South Africa), received an MBA from the University of Oxford in 2019 and is a registered systems practitioner. Through poetry, writing and facilitation, he advocates for rewilding the human spirit and embodied stewardship of nature.

But Jane happened to look round, and happened to
smile: it was decided. He placed himself by her.

The Jane Austen Festival

The View from Bath
Rachel Beswick

The honey-coloured Bath stone of Great Pulteney Street glows under the warm autumn sun. A top-hatted gentleman and bonneted lady stroll along the pavement, past groups of young ladies, the ribbons on their empire-line dresses fluttering in the breeze. Across the road, a group of red-coated soldiers laugh and joke together.

It was doubtless a sight that Austen herself saw during her time living in Bath; it could just as well be a scene from one of the novels she set in the city; it could even be a scene from one of the many film or television adaptations of Austen's work.

However, it is a normal September weekend in modern-day Bath: the Jane Austen Festival is in town!

First held in the year 2000, the Jane Austen Festival has grown from a few events over an autumn weekend to 200 events over ten days every September, attended by Austen fans of all sorts, from all over the world.

While balls and soirées are the events most in demand, the Jane Austen Festival has something for every type of Jane Austen lover. There are talks and lectures, dances and parties, promenades and walking tours, fencing, croquet and archery, book clubs and film-screenings.

There is no one typical Jane Austen Festival-attendee. The Festival prides itself on providing a warm welcome and ample entertainment for everyone who loves Austen's books, all those who love the film or television versions of her works, those

The Jane Austen Festival

who love Regency history and those who love the stunning Georgian city of Bath.

Comments such as "A dream come true!" and "The best ten days of my year!" are what motivate the team of festival organisers and volunteers to wade through the paperwork and the emails necessary to organise hundreds of events over dozens of locations.

A question which is often asked is why so many people still want to celebrate Jane Austen, her characters and her creations, 250 years after her birth. While the elegant dress of her time and the magnificent locations of her stories – real and imagined – probably help, ultimately it is the people Austen depicts that keep drawing fans to her, decade after decade. The characters that inspired Austen during her time in Bath still walk along the Royal Crescent or Great Pulteney Street today: people who are funny and flawed; people who put others down and people who build others up; people who can laugh at themselves; people who plot and scheme; people who change for the better.

Austen's great power is in capturing human nature – we have all encountered the kind of characters she brings to life on the page, and so we keep returning to her stories again and again, whether that be with a book, audiobook, film or television series.

www.janeausten.co.uk

The Jane Austen Festival is held annually in September, in the beautiful Georgian city of Bath, Somerset, UK. It is run by a small, all-female team, ably assisted by dozens of wonderfully skilled volunteers who come from all over the world to help celebrate Austen's works, life and times.

Encounters with Jane Austen

Above: Volunteers at the Jane Austen Festival in Bath. Photo: Jane Austen Festival
Below: The Royal Crescent, Bath. Photo: Ellen Cheshire

Austen's World

Above: Chawton Cottage, near Alton in Hampshire. Photo: Ellen Cheshire
Below: Dining Room at Chawton Cottage. Photo: Cheryl Robson

Jane Austen's pedestal writing table at Chawton Cottage
(Jane Austen House)
Photo: Cheryl Robson

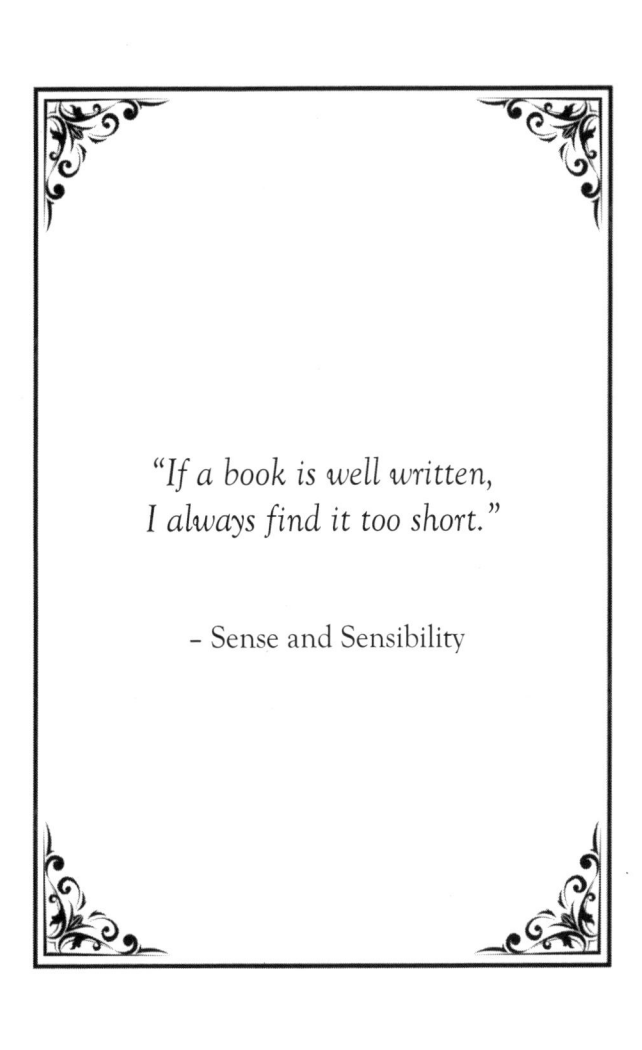

*"If a book is well written,
I always find it too short."*

– Sense and Sensibility

Great Fiction to read:

Volta by Nikki Dudley
ISBN 978-1-912430-55-0 Price £9.99

Bone Rites by Natalie Bayley
ISBN 978-1-912430-87-1 Price £11.99

Pomegranate Sky by Louise Soraya Black
ISBN 978-1-906582-10-4 Price £8.99

Shambala Junction by Dipika Mukherjee
ISBN 978-1-910798-39-3 Price £9.99

The River's Song by Suchen Christine Lim
ISBN 978-1-9006582-98-2 Price £9.99

Sacred by Eliette Abecassis
ISBN 978-0-9536757-8-4 Price £9.95

Intelligent Non-Fiction to read:

Virginia Woolf in Richmond by Peter Fullagar
ISBN 978-1-913641-28-3 Price £16.99

Unravelling Women's Art by PL Henderson
ISBN 978-1-913641-15-3 Price £19.99

50 Women Sculptors ed Cheryl Robson
ISBN 978-0-993220-77-7 Price £24.99

Art, Theatre & Women's Suffrage by Irene Cockroft
& Susan Croft ISBN 978-1-906582-08-1 Price £9.99

The Original Suffrage Cookbook ed LO Kleber
ISBN 978-1-912430-13-0 Price £12.99

The Women Writers Handbook ed Ann Sandham
ISBN 978-1-912430-33-8 Price £14.99

Virginia's Sisters edited by Gabi Reigh
ISBN 978-1-912430-78-9 £16.99

**For more great books
www.aurorametro.com**